# Alaska Hoops

# Coaching Tips & Tales

# from the Girls' Locker Room

Becky Crabtree

Illustrated by Papi Crabtree

ISBN: 978-1-888215-11-3
Library of Congress Control Number: 2009928355

A number of the chapters from Alaska Hoops were published statewide by Alaska Newspapers in recent years.

United States of America
Fathom Publishing Company
PO Box 200448
Anchorage, AK 99520-0448
www.alaskahoops.com
2009

# Dedication

These stories are dedicated to the memory of the women who were the ballplayers of the past including my mother, Rachel B. Hatcher, and the young women of Alaska who will be the ballplayers of the future, particularly Miss Vanessa Grace.

# Acknowledgements

Many people contributed to the writing of this book:

Special thanks go to friends, family members, and those who work "out the road" in Barrow who listened to these stories before they were written down.

This book would not have been possible without the encouragement and editing of my friend and teacher, Jay St. Vincent. Likewise, the patience and persistence of Connie Taylor from Fathom Publishing is appreciated

Finally, I would like to express my gratitude and affection to my ballplayers: the 1993-2004 Lady Wolves of Hopson Middle School and, most especially, to the 2005 and 2006 Lady Whalers of Barrow High School. Writing this book was the only way I could bear leaving you. Thanks for the memories!

# Table of Contents


Introduction . . . . . . . . . . . . . . . . . . . . . . . . . . . . . . . . . . . .1

The Alaskan Dance . . . . . . . . . . . . . . . . . . . . . . . . . . . . . .5

Grin and Bear It . . . . . . . . . . . . . . . . . . . . . . . . . . . . . . . 10

Way Too Young to Play this Old . . . . . . . . . . . . . . . . . . 14

Coaching Choices . . . . . . . . . . . . . . . . . . . . . . . . . . . . . 18

Superstitions . . . . . . . . . . . . . . . . . . . . . . . . . . . . . . . . 21

The Night the Ancients Danced . . . . . . . . . . . . . . . . . . 26

Basketball as an Art Form . . . . . . . . . . . . . . . . . . . . . . 31

School Politics:
Never Cut the Secretary's Daughter . . . . . . . . . . . . . . . 35

Ice Cream Classic . . . . . . . . . . . . . . . . . . . . . . . . . . . . . 39

Electronics . . . . . . . . . . . . . . . . . . . . . . . . . . . . . . . . . . 43

Differences in the Huddle . . . . . . . . . . . . . . . . . . . . . . . 47

Band of Sisters . . . . . . . . . . . . . . . . . . . . . . . . . . . . . . . 51

Consider the Source . . . . . . . . . . . . . . . . . . . . . . . . . . . 55

The Last Frontier . . . . . . . . . . . . . . . . . . . . . . . . . . . . . 59

Coach of the Year . . . . . . . . . . . . . . . . . . . . . . . . . . . . . 63

State! . . . . . . . . . . . . . . . . . . . . . . . . . . . . . . . . . . . . . . 66

Lilly . . . . . . . . . . . . . . . . . . . . . . . . . . . . . . . . . . . . . . . 70

Little Dribblers . . . . . . . . . . . . . . . . . . . . . . . . . . . . . . . 74

Letter to Mom . . . . . . . . . . . . . . . . . . . . . . . . . . . . . . . 79

Compassion . . . . . . . . . . . . . . . . . . . . . . . . . . . . . . . . . 82

Epiphany . . . . . . . . . . . . . . . . . . . . . . . . . . . . . . . . . . . 86

# Introduction

I have two early memories that still summon up total bewilderment. When I was three years old, I helped pick hot banana peppers in the garden and then rubbed both eyes. The burning was intense and unexplainable to me at that tender age. A year or two later, I discovered that a basketball would not bounce straight when it hit the tufts of grass around the worn dirt spot in the pasture field. Too young to realize that the dirt oval was located in front of the hay stack pole that held the backboard and rim, all I knew was that my brothers bounced a basketball smoothly there.

At least the dribbling appeared to be smooth as I watched between the slats in the gate just outside the yard, the boundary of my world. As an only daughter among three sons, there were limitations set especially for me. I'd sneak though the gate when no one was looking and try to imitate the dribbling, but the ball would not cooperate. I didn't get it. I didn't scream like I did with the peppers, but I wasn't a bit happy until I figured out that the ground under a bounce had to be smooth or the ball could go anywhere. I guess I've been a basketball geek for a long time.

In junior high school, I carried a basketball with me on the bus to Glenwood School near Princeton, West Virginia where there were larger, smoother dirt spots on the playground. The other kids let me play if I owned the ball, so I begged for one on my 12th birthday. If I could've left my body and watched back then, I think I would've seen a lonely, knobby-kneed adolescent girl carrying books in one arm and a basketball in the other.

At this age, I loved to listen to games on the radio and keep my own score sheets and check them at halftime as the announcer read the stats. When I got to see a game, I was enthralled. It was so beautiful, like sailboats floating on a lake or a ballet. There was so much to watch, so many side-plots to the scoring part of the game.

In high school, I played on the mighty Tigerette team. No, we were not Lady Tigers like today's team and there were not five of us on a team, but six. In the late 1960s young women were not supposed to overtax their body by running full court, so a team consisted of two defensive players that stayed in the backcourt, two that played only in the front court, and two rovers who could play full court. We wore gym suits that had numbers stenciled on with stinky permanent markers. In my mental videos of those days, I sense our exhilarating memories of running "coast to coast" and maddening, screaming skid marks from our Keds when we had to stop at half court. It just galled me to play defense or offense as opposed to roving. Once I boldly announced that I'd "rather sit on the bench than play half court" and earned the chance to learn that it wasn't true. Then and now, I believed playing ball on any terms beats not playing at all.

I chose a girls' college for one reason: the gym didn't have to be shared with the men's team. Tiny Virginia Intermont College in Bristol, Virginia offered the world to me – a gym available night or day, a basketball team (of five) that traveled and had real uniforms and basketball clinics at the University of Tennessee, only a half day's drive away. After three years of pre-med, I applied to medical school and took a graduate level test to qualify. At my interview, I was told that there would be 76 students selected for medical school admission that year and 5 of them would be women. The five highest scores on the entrance exam earned by females would get to attend. Reacting quickly, I asked the interviewing committee what happened if the sixth ranking female's score was higher than the 71$^{st}$ male. I was not accepted for admission that year and never reapplied. I had enough science and physical education classes for a teaching certificate so I transferred to Bluefield State College where I spent another three semesters to finish an education degree.

While shooting around in the huge gymnasium there, I met two ball-playing characters from just over the mountain, Peanut and Roger. They both treated me like an equal on the court and off. I first dated one and then fell in love with the other. My previous vow to never marry was forgotten and Roger and I tied the knot. I am entranced by the cathedral-like quality of gyms and wanted to get married at center court in the Bluefield State practice gym, but my proper mother took her bed. Instead, we got married in the front yard.

I taught school in three counties of southern West Virginia, had three daughters, and coached three sports during the first fourteen years of marriage. In those years, I learned that hard work on the court didn't always equal victories, that women didn't get paid the same for the same job, and that girls needed role models to show them that they were as valuable as boys. I reffed, I played on women's teams and I coached, sometimes huge with an unborn daughter on board, and sometimes with a baby in the bleachers.

Our family had growing pains and financial woes, so we accepted and fulfilled a two-year teaching contract on Guam. By then daughter #2, Katie was playing middle school basketball and Roger and I were both actively playing ball with our church there and coaching at Upi Elementary School. From there, we borrowed sweaters from Air Force friends and went to Anchorage for the teacher job fair. We were hired in Barrow. I was a good fit there. I loved the basketball mania that consumed the village every winter and coached Little Dribblers, middle school and varsity high school basketball. The best and worst moments of my coaching career all happened in my fifteen years as a teacher and coach in Barrow.

I see few women willing to brave the Barrow politics and abuse hurled on coaches, including myself. In a world where a career in public education is one of the most underappreciated and underpaid, the plight of a coach is even more difficult. Women coaches often suffer from isolation in addition to the stresses of the job. In an Alaskan town suffering from social ills, the role of a coach can become quite intense.

Today, I live in the village of Atqasuk, Alaska, sixty miles from Barrow. I expect that my new acquaintances here do not see anything athletic in my slow, plump body. They probably don't know how much I love basketball yet. I hope that they will notice the grin that lights up my face when it is time for basketball practice or the frown when I am trying to figure out the nuances of the game. Even after 50 years of basketball fascination, I can't wait to coach a new group of Alaskan ballplayers!

Becky Crabtree
November 2008

# The Alaskan Dance

Even though basketball was invented far from Bush Alaska in a time before I was born (an unbelievably long time ago to my students), it is firmly embedded in the culture of small Alaskan communities here and now. In remote small villages like Barrow, recreational opportunities are limited and indoor space is at a premium during the long winter. Basketball has long been my favorite sport, but it also reigns as the sport of choice for a majority of residents here – toddlers to senior citizens.

Shortened basketball hoops, about four feet high, are part of the playground equipment for three- and four-year-old classrooms. Even at their tender ages, they wear NBA jerseys and are aware of the antics of the pros as well as their moms and dads who play city league basketball and big brothers and sisters who play for the Barrow Whalers. Hanging on the rim after dunking the ball persists as the number one safety hazard during pre-school playtime. In addition to the universal chase and tag games of older elementary students, dribbling, shooting, and scrimmaging are part of indoor recess play.

The basketball league for the youngest athletes is called Little Dribblers. It is organized by Recreation Departments in each village and takes place in city and school gyms, in Barrow called Piuraagvik (Inupiat for a place to play). The five-month season is propelled by the heroic volunteer efforts of parents and basketball devotees. Players compete either in a junior division of second and third graders or a senior division of fourth and fifth graders. The senior teams compete with other village teams which require an airplane ride since no roads connect any villages. In the springtime, two teams from each of seven North Slope villages fly to Barrow for the annual Little Dribbler tournament. Over a hundred nine- and ten-year-olds sleeping on the gym floors, eating in the bleachers, hanging out

with classmates and cousins and watching and playing basketball all day long. Pre-teen paradise!

Most middle schools field an intramural basketball program. At Hopson Middle School about a dozen teams make up the program. The school has an enrollment of 250 students; when I taught there nearly 200 of them participated. Rules are modified to insure that the program helps develop skills and love of the sport: Every player must play in every game. Three point shots are not allowed so teamwork can be emphasized and young arms can grow stronger. Zone defense is not permitted in hopes that players will learn to think about defense and move with the opponent that they are guarding. Finally, a full court press is not allowed until the last two minutes of each half so that competitors can learn to dribble in the back court without fear of attack.

The middle school also fields a varsity and junior varsity team for girls and for boys. To have a season, coaches must find other middle school teams willing to play, earn the necessary funds for airfare, and spend nights sleeping in classrooms and churches to play as many games as possible in one week-long trip. The trip costs upwards of $20,000 every year.

Every village on the North Slope has a boys and girls high school varsity basketball team. Some have junior varsity teams. The school budget in past years for the Barrow High basketball program has been a significant amount of money. Airfare remains a huge expense not only for Barrow kids traveling to play other schools, but also for the teams that come to Barrow. Barrow pays their expenses so that home games can be played. A Barrow Boosters Club exists to help cover additional expenses. Current spending is much less and high school teams have recently missed as much as two weeks of school to play several games using only one airplane ticket, thus saving money.

The gym is standing room only for most home games. Two junior varsity games and two varsity games are played on Friday and Saturday nights to maximize income as well as game experience for the players. The crowd is loyal, vocal, and often creates and organizes their own cheers without the benefit of the leadership of uniformed cheerleaders. The band plays, spectators visit between games and during timeouts, 50/50 drawings and cake raffles are held at halftime. The hallways are lined with vendors selling items as varied as caribou with rice to

snow cones to Whaler t-shirts. Each night of basketball is a festive community event.

Fans gather around the radio to keep up with games played "on the road." Usually, the local radio station KBRW broadcasts all away games. When there was a glitch in the radio service at one away game, a fan attending the games borrowed a cell phone to report the score at each quarter to the radio station so reports could be made on the air. The radio announcer also serves as the city recreation director. He has both a distinctive voice and first hand knowledge of all the high school basketball players since they were Little Dribblers.

On their eighteenth birthday, players become eligible to play on City League teams. This colorful collection of teams represents different cultures and professions as well as some groups with no common affiliations like the Screaming Lemmings, the Snowy Owls, and the Rebels. Some players are fiercely competitive; some are simply looking for exercise. Games are usually squeezed into a full gym schedule twice a week, late in the evening, the final game beginning at 10 PM. Tournaments are held all through the year, like the Fall Turkey Tournament in which each winner gets a frozen turkey and each player on the runner-up team gets a bag of stuffing.

On Sunday mornings, the over-fifty league plays at Piuraagvik. Much less formal than the other city league programs, teams are chosen by shooting from the top of the key, the first five that hit the shot play on the same team. Winning team members continue to play until they can't run any more.

Basketball is not the only sport in the villages. Schools have swimming pools. Cross-country coaches usually exert effort to have enough runners for a team. There are interscholastic teams and adult leagues for volleyball. Barrow High has offered a football program recently and smaller schools have introduced flag football teams. Native games are taught and students regularly participate in international contests and the Christmas games. Wrestling aficionados declare the superiority of that sport and have a following. The city has a hockey rink and there is an organization overseeing hockey and curling. The recreation department also promotes soccer, flag football, and softball, but the popularity of basketball leads all other sports.

Basketball fans from all over the state pour into Anchorage for the "Great Alaskan Shoot-out." College teams invade the University of Alaska gym during the week of Thanksgiving and

village classrooms empty as students travel with their families to town for the games. Often these are the same students who try to head their homework paper with the number on their jersey instead of their name. Similarly, Anchorage hotels fill in March for the state tournament for high school teams – a weeklong event that involves hundreds of players and thousands of fans.

Why does basketball draw so many players and fans in rural Alaska? Does it engage so many because it is played indoors in a cold land? Is it because the game has been around for generations? Does the immediate gratification of seeing a shot rip the net attract players? Is it simply an exciting game? I think that basketball is important to the people here because it incorporates the same values as those of the culture that has survived the harsh conditions of the Arctic. The values of the Inupiaq people: cooperation, respect, compassion, and sharing, are all present on the basketball court and behind the scenes, supporting those who coach and play the game.

Years ago, as a gym aide during evening recreation at the middle school gym, I was shocked to see everyone playing at the same time. The better players had a full court game in progress while half court games were going at each of the four side goals. Toddlers wobbled around the sidelines and small children rolled and bounced full size basketballs just beyond the base lines. Sometimes, a Frisbee or football floated above all the chaos when youngsters stationed in corners of the gym played catch above the teeming life on the court. Every now then a kid on roller skates glided through. A sweaty mist permeated the air. I could just taste the saltiness on the tip of my tongue. My mind could barely comprehend all the activity. At first, I alternately swore and prayed nervously under my breath anticipating injuries any moment, but they were amazingly few. The room throbbed with life – I couldn't be sure if it was driven by laughter or the beat of balls bouncing or pounding heartbeats. This seemingly divine choreography allows for maximum use of a space without much danger. During a fast break in the big game, a player will stop and return a stray ball to the game of a younger child. Tiny children learn to dodge the movement of bigger boys and girls. When

participants in one game take a break the space they just occupied is consumed by others until the athletes return from the water fountain and resume play. This Alaskan dance fills the gym in every village on the North Slope.

The contemporary t-shirt slogan: "Basketball is life. The rest is just details." nails the feeling precisely. I hope the corporate promoter who came up with it has been able to leave the office cubicle and experience the total joy of Alaskan basketball.

*Coaching Tip*
*Recognize the significance of basketball*
*to the community.*

# Grin and Bear It

The boys' high school basketball team from a tiny bush village had outscored every team they played all season, winning each game by more than thirty points. They frequently shot left-handed during second half to help the other team's chances. Scrubs played a lot. At season's end, they blew through regional competition like an Adak windstorm. Over and over as the state tournament grew near, the coach told the boys, his colleagues, and the fans, "It's in the bag." He used the week of practice before state to prepare the players for carrying him off the court on their shoulders after the final victory. Inexplicably, the team didn't play well at state. They lost the championship by 22 points. Years later, he still hears "Is it in the bag?" about once a week from former players and old friends as they greet him.

There would be a lot less laughter during the Alaska basketball season if coaches could prepare for everything. On the court and off, unexpected events tweak our funny bones. The more important the situation, the funnier unforeseen happenings appear. Sometimes it takes a while for the humor to become obvious to those involved, but the best policy is to laugh loud and long.

Traveling can be full of surprises. Forgetting the uniforms can be a real hoot. So can locking the keys in the team van or getting lost on the way to the game. Sleeping on basketball trips is vital, however, and thus, gets really funny.

During one four-night stay for regionals at Bethel High School, I planned to sleep in a classroom assigned to my players. We had finally settled into our inflatable mattresses and I was glad to have my newly purchased blow-up Coleman bed between me and the cold floor. I checked the girls and was prepared for a long winter's nap when I heard it – the sound that would control my well being for the next four nights. First, I tried to block the hole with duct tape using a flashlight to see

and feeling for the tiny hole with my fingertips. That didn't work. Next, I drug my suitcase into the hallway to find a bicycle tire patch kit. More repair by flashlight in the room. That didn't work either. Finally, I turned on the lights and borrowed superglue from a sleepy girl. I nearly glued my fingers to the mattress, but didn't plug the hole. The mattress had to be re-inflated every two hours to keep my tired old bones off the cold floor. The pump was so loud that it woke everyone else in the room, so for four long nights, I carried the mattress into the hallway and aired it up every two hours. It wasn't amusing until much, much later.

When a girls' team stays in the same hotel as a boys' team, interaction is inevitable. One year, while staying at a nice hotel in Anchorage with a courtyard, high school boys were staying in rooms which were in sight of the Barrow girls' rooms. Teenagers being teenagers, the boys wanted to gain the girls' attention. The senior boys made up some water balloons which they stored outside on their room's balcony. Later in the evening, the boys planned to toss the water balloons at the sliding doors of the girls' rooms. Sounds like an innocent good time, right? The balloons had frozen solid. The toss across the courtyard had enough force behind it to shatter the six and a half foot high glass door leading to the girls' suite. Glass flew everywhere. Damages were over a thousand dollars. The senior boy was sent home but the look on his face at contact was priceless, at least according to the girls peeking at him from another window when it happened.

Some small funnies happen on the court because the players (or referees) are confused. Jumpers facing the wrong direction for the opening tip is a classic mistake. So is a player going the wrong direction just after the tip. When the first goal is scored for the opposite team it seems quite funny for the recipients of the points, but not so funny for those who made the mistake. Similarly, confused players guard the defense by mistake when their team has the ball or don't play defense because they think their team is on offense. Usually, a lot of yelling takes place before anyone smiles.

The warm up time before the game is prime ground for hilarity, partly because players attempt to convey an impression of poise. Most home teams that have run through a paper-covered hoop to enter the gym have a story about tripping on the hoop and falling. Therefore, Tina, a petite team leader at Hopson Middle School, was warned by her coach to

jump high enough through the hoop so she wouldn't trip. Tina listened intently, remembered at the right moment, and jumped so high that she bumped her head on the top of the hoop and fell forward; the rest of her team tumbled through and piled up on top of her: a new technique for the same funny scene.

Another self-assured high school player, Judy, with perfectly styled hair and make-up, shot a lay-up during the warm-up and turned back with a serious look to see if it went in. Still running, she collided head-on with the older, sweaty custodian sweeping the end of the gym, knocked him on his back spread-eagled and landed on top of him knocking the broom onto the court. Some of her teammates had to leave the court to compose themselves.

During a home game, a wiry tenth grader named Kary made a mistake that would haunt her for many years. She was a sub who spent a lot of time on the bench. When the coach called her to quickly go in, she dramatically ripped off her tear-away warm-up pants to report to the scorer's table. The crowd got a glimpse of bare legs, but the girls on the bench also got a good look at Wonder Woman across the rear of her pink panties. Supposedly, it was her good luck underwear. She had forgotten to put on her uniform shorts under the warm-ups.

Unfortunately, physical pain also elicits smiles. When anyone is surprised by being hit by the ball, there is laughter. A middle school cheerleader, paying attention to the fans in the back row of the bleachers turned back to watch the game at the instant after a hard pass was thrown in her direction. There was no time to escape. The basketball boinked her full in the face. It had to hurt, but spectators turned their heads to hide smiles. More laughs echo through the gym when the ball hits a player and remains in play. I watched a hyperactive high school junior varsity boy spin around and around in frustration to find the ball which had just bounced high into the air off the top of his head. Another player had the advantage of perspective and likely, a non-throbbing head. He caught the ball and scored. In another miscue, Rosemary was ahead of the team on a fast break in perfect position to catch a pass and score when she chose the wrong moment to look ahead instead of at the ball which whacked her on the back with a thud. The other team picked it up and reversed the action.

The shock when a player gets hit in the face by the ball registers on their expression for a few seconds longer than the ball. Spectators flinch and grin. Once, a large girl was guarding

the player with the ball closely. Part of her defense was to talk to her opponent, taunting her with inflammatory phrases, "You're not going anywhere ..." "Not in my house!" "Nothing there for you." Undersized and perturbed, the smaller player tried to heave the ball hard down the court. It slammed the big girl right in the nose and must have momentarily numbed it. She screamed, "My nose is gone!" as she ran to the sideline feeling for her face.

Sometimes the laughter is restricted to the locker room. After an intense game that was won by a single point, the key player on the winning team shook hands with the other team dejectedly. She then covered her head with a towel, sat in the wet floor of the smelly locker room and cried. Teammates flocked to her side, squeezed her shoulders and rubbed her back. Wrenching sobs were the only sounds coming out from under the towel. She refused to be consoled. Twenty minutes later, while reviewing the scorebook her friends finally got through her funk to figure it out. She thought her team had lost by one point and it was her fault. Even she had to chuckle through her tears at the mistake.

Research does not conclusively show that those who laugh have less stress and live longer, but it is clear that those who laugh have fun. Surprises that upset the ritual and formality of basketball provide endless possibilities for hilarity. Remember that games are supposed to be fun and have a ball this season!!

*Coaching Tip*
*Keep your sense of humor handy.*

# Way Too Young to Play this Old

For a few who allow basketball into their lives, it has the potential to be absorbed into the bloodstream like an addiction. The thumping of a basketball on the gym floor echoes in the pulse of these players. Their craving to play leads them to the gym. Frequent suffering in the form of jammed fingers, floor burns, split lips, scratches, and rolled ankles do not distract from their quest to stay in the game. Often, these are veteran players. They have spent years of their lives performing for a crowd of hometown fans. The feeling of being cheered on by fans can be heady stuff. The user wants the high to go on forever. It sure beats the adult workday world where cheers are rare and the score is never clear.

However, there is a real obstacle to immortality on the court: maturity of the body. Not the kind that creates curves on young women and facial hair on young men, but the maturity that seems to occur in the forty-somethingth year of life. Besides the well-known facts of human anatomy learned in health class, there are mysterious developments which science hasn't prepared us for. Shocking physiological and psychological changes are imminent in the fifth decade of life. As various qualities of maturity begin to appear, mind and body start to separate. I can confirm this process because I have lived through it.

Against my better judgment, I re-entered the city league arena after a full life of playing and coaching. I had felt the arrival of maturity a decade before, in my early forties, but was lured back (see paragraph 1). All the reminders of my advancing age have come flashing back.

I felt the early onset of maturity while trying to run. It's harder! In fact, my first indication of maturing may be the realization that I just can't keep up. My gym bag contains knee braces, adhesive tape, and ankle wraps. It reeks with the medicinal minty aroma of "Icy Hot." The Alaskan joke that you

are safe from a bear attack if you can outrun just one person from your group applies here. I figure that I don't have to get down the floor faster than all my teammates, just one of them. This keeps the attention off my lagging behind (pun intended).

Twenty years ago, I was a scrappy player who dove and hit the floor to grab any loose ball, who sacrificed my body to save the ball from going out of bounds, or stood strong to take a charge. Not anymore. I now avoid all opportunities for physical contact. The subconscious surely stores memories of lingering pain the day after the great fun of being on the court. The brain neurons, old or not, still recall the peak time of soreness, that tender second day after the activity.

The first day after a lot of running, life rolls on with little twinges here and there. I can still ascend or descend the stairs. I can get up from chairs without assistance. The second day, I must hold the rail and grit my teeth to get up the steps and going downstairs is even worse. It hurts to comb my hair. To rise from a seated position, I must use an arm to brace my weight. I've learned to bring everything I need to the recliner where I sit for the evening.

Phase two of maturity is paralysis. I can see the ball rolling on the floor and my eyes send signals to the body, but by the time my arms and legs get the signals it is too late for action. The ball can be heading out of bounds and I know in my head to take a couple of quick steps to get it, but I don't do it. My mind leads but my feet don't follow. A colleague told about the time he was rebounding from the front of the rim, had an open lane for an outlet pass and by the time he grabbed the ball and turned, it was, amazingly, too late. Everything had shifted on the court in the time it took him to perform the simple act. Perhaps this freeze-up is caused by mature brains that subconsciously remember the pain that may follow quick movement. This immobility on the court surprised me the first time. I still knew where to go but I couldn't get to the place I knew I should be. Like an imbecile, I stood in the front court grinning in disbelief.

Ball handling skills go next. I've dribbled the ball up the court thousands of times and swear that something possesses my fingertips. My aging palms slap against the ball crazily like beginners just learning the skill. Look closely and you will see folks my age glance at their hand like a baby who just noticed the attachment of fingers. Behind the back passes and between the legs dribbling have both become the stuff of memories.

My offense becomes limited to passing and spot up shooting. I totally avoid fast break participation. Previous signature moves are gone from my physical repertoire. There is no jumping. It is important to block out opponents as far from the goal as possible so the ball has time to fall lower so I have a chance to get it. Shooting from outside also seems more practical.

Defensively, it just doesn't seem so important when the other team scores. My husband adds that if you are wondering if your knees are going to give way, you are more careful about the steps you take to guard others. He compares his defensive shuffle to the stiff-legged gait of Fred Sanford. Old people don't play point on defense – we need to be in the middle or the back of a zone.

Along with physical changes come new attitudes. When I played on a school team, back when the world was young, I wanted to play the entire game, every game. This has changed. In more recent years, the burning of my throat has been one signal that it was time to sit down and gulp some water to put out the fire in my mouth. Total limpness of my legs is a second signal that I need to go to the bench. Muscle aches lead me to the sideline and it's a good guess that if I am buckled over with hands on knees, it's time to sit down. I've learned that it is not good to play so much after spots of light appear before your eyes, either. There are other reasons to get a substitute. I like to adjust the ankle brace hidden under my sock every now and then, to visit with other players about the hideous uniforms of our opponents, or to quietly flex my muscles to be sure nothing is broken. And sometimes, even during a game, I need to go to the bathroom. A solid hit from an elbow or the ball is difficult for older bladders to absorb.

My fierce competitive spirit has mellowed to the joy of recreation: time with other humans away from television and computer screens is more valuable than winning. Disdain of substitutes is replaced by my pitiful, pleading look towards the bench. A chance to sit and recover a normal heart rate weighs in more importantly than the youthful pride of finishing a game. The running clock, once scorned, is now welcomed. A teammate told me that as we lose our seriousness about competition, we are entering a different level of basketball. Sounds good to me.

Those who can't move quickly position themselves in the best location for a rebound – they can remember where missed shots are going. Players who may get too tired to play need to

warm up with less intensity. The smart senior athlete will not be dunking or galloping around the court during warm-up time. They need to hydrate often and save some energy for the game. Individuals who feel their touch on the ball fading must practice shooting specifically from the spot where they are most likely to be open. Muscles can be trained at any age. Setting screens is a specialty on offense that frees up a younger shooter. Finally, the relief of a hot bath after exertion may compensate for some of the pain.

At this point in life, I thought I understood my own body, but I had to reach back into the past to remember the tips coaches had given me: Warm up before playing. Drink lots of fluids. Eat right. Sleep enough. Don't smoke. Don't drink. Give everyone a chance to play. Compensate for your weaknesses with your strengths. Ah, inspiration ... the influence of a coach never ends.

My similarly aged friends and I have argued whether or not our bodies slow down because of age. Some think that the lack of activity causes the deterioration, basically that bodies slow down because they quit moving not because they are older. Roland, in his late sixties, exemplifies the theory that the body does what you train it to do. He works out several times a week and plays ball at least twice. His fitness shames slower players who are younger by decades. There are frequent injuries in the Sunday morning league, but Roland never gets hurt. I, conversely, am a good example of inactivity and extra pounds weakening my skills. Age must have something to do with my ineptness!

I figure the love of the game is as powerful as the treachery of old age. Those, like myself, who can't beat the need for round ball with other activities and aren't quite ready for the Scooter Store are finding a kind team who will let them play (Thank you, team Geode and coach Crystal!) or an over-the-hill league, packing the painkiller and liniment and hobbling on over to the local gym.

*Coaching Tip*
*Take care of yourself*
*– you may get suckered in for the long haul.*

# Coaching Choices

How could Piggy and Princess not be best friends? They were two little girls in the same grade, both transplanted to rural Alaska from South Pacific heritages via Anchorage, and both exceptional basketball players.

Princess lived with her dad and her older brother. Mom had moved to Anchorage after the divorce and was raising a second family there. Dad was a facilities manager and a cab driver in Barrow and was devoted to both his children. He had a strong accent and epitomized the hard-working, ever smiling Filipino resident well known in Barrow. When her dad travelled on basketball trips, his dad brought Princess along and she slept in the room with the girls' team. At home games her dad sat in the same spot in the bleachers for years watching his offspring dazzle the fans. He seldom spoke and the one time he offered advice to me, it was done quietly, in private, after much consideration. Near the end of the season, he said, "Princess is tired." And he was right. On the court, Princess was expressionless, but after a game, she relaxed with lots of laughter and loudness.

Piggy, born third youngest of eight siblings in a Samoan family, had the devotion of both parents and that of a houseful of brothers and sisters. Although she wasn't the youngest, she had qualities usually found in the baby of the family. She was the center of attention from parents and her siblings, both positive and negative. She was an undisputed star and crowd pleaser during a game. Her parents were also devoted to their children and were present in the gym for every contest. They had plenty of advice to give to coaches and to Piggy during the game and were not shy about broadcasting their opinions

afterwards. Piggy's emotions were transparent on the court but after a game she was often quiet and moody. Even though she played spectacularly, her friendship with teammates was strained because she demanded that those on the team perform up to her expectations. All except for the closeness with Princess, who was ever her equal.

They were a formidable duo on the court. Tiny Princess could fly down the floor for a fast break, and sturdier Piggy could throw a baseball pass with a basketball as accurately as a grown man by the time she was in sixth grade. One of them was usually the high scorer and the other was usually the second highest scorer. In middle school, they appeared to have internal radar for each other on offense. No-look passes, lobs, thread the needle pitches, and chucking the ball from end to end of the court to one another were ordinary events. They could both shoot threes and they were both dangerous driving to the basket. Both dark-haired girls led the team but with very different leadership styles.

By the end of their eighth grade (and undefeated) season, these skills had me in a quandary. There was one award for the Most Valuable Player of the year. My unpleasant job was to choose one of them to receive it.

There is more than one uncomfortable coaching choice to be made in adolescent athletics. In addition to announcing individual awards to participants in a team sport, every season I dreaded "the cut," the horrible procedure that excludes young players from the team. Yes, limiting the team roster has a logical basis. There are only so many uniforms, so many seats on the bench, and so much time and space to practice. I am one of the evil adults who trusted these reasons to cut team members to a manageable number.

In sixth grade, Serena lay stretched out in the back hallway sobbing and screaming after she didn't make the JV team. Cynthia quit coming to school when she didn't make the team. One mother wrote me that her daughter, Rhoda, would never pick up a basketball again since she didn't advance beyond the try-outs. Some of these girls had never before been refused anything they wanted and  although they needed to be refused something in their young lives, this was not the best situation.

Now, after years of selecting teams, I can better see that the life-changing ramifications of "the cut" to youngsters overshadow any organizational value to their coaches. I may have developed the thinking of parents who want all the children they can physically have: "We will find a way to clothe them all and pay attention to them all and support them. It is the right thing to do!" I do believe that young people that want to play sports should have the chance. There should be two teams or an intramural program or a city league in addition to the school league. They all need to play!

With the same sense of righteousness, I could not easily select a MVP. I compared stats. Scoring was similar, assists were roughly equal, and rebounding numbers matched. Both girls had stolen the ball many times, both had few turnovers. Both shot blisteringly high percentages of free throws. When I visualized giving the prize to one or the other of them, I knew the other girl would hug the winner and congratulate her. Neither would begrudge the trophy if her best friend won it.

The presentation was to be made at the end of season pot luck dinner and the parents were already assembling in the school cafeteria before I made my decision. I determined that it was wrong to choose between the two best players and designate one over the other. So, I slipped away to the school's wood shop before dinner.

At the climax of the evening after the meal, I felt right and ready as I announced, "The Most Valuable Player Award for the Lady Wolves this season goes to not one, but two distinguished players." and presented both Piggy and Princess half of the wooden plaque. They smiled and hugged amid cheers of parents and friends.

Years have passed and both girls have won their share of more important trophies, both have a state championship medal, and both are likely to excel in competitive college basketball. I hope when they see a small brown chunk of wood tossed in a box in the back of a closet, they remember a moment from childhood when they could not be set apart by the coach who prized them both.

*Coaching Tip*
*Break with tradition when necessary.*

# Superstitions

In addition to practicing, strategizing, analyzing data, and scouting the other team, coaches and players in my life have employed a range of superstitions to help ensure victory. None of the Alaskan rituals are as extreme as Ecuador's soccer team. They hired a mystic to shoo away evil spirits in each of the 12 stadiums used in the World Cup. However, they do illustrate that no matter how skilled the participant, they all want an edge on winning.

Some practices are disgusting. A hockey playing friend says he doesn't wash his gear. Ever. A football coaching colleague says that, on his college team, the quarterback wore a garment that belonged to his girlfriend. I don't want to know which garment. A middle school boy wore his wrestling singlet day and night the week before a match. He may have won because his opponent couldn't stand to stay close enough to him to wrestle.

A ritual is practical when the superstition also improves the believer's looks. My daughter thought that knee socks were lucky during her high school basketball years, but she also thought they made her calves look "hot." Several years ago, Sarah Villalon, a Lady Whaler from Barrow, meticulously ironed her uniform before every game. Other players wore wrist bands and head bands "because they were lucky," but the wearers generally spent time in front of the mirror admiring the look, too. High school athletes can't afford to wear a new pair of shoes every game like Michael Jordan, but we had a player from the South Pacific that had to have something new for every game – shoelaces, a scrunchie, or just a new tissue tucked in her sock, like the "something old, something new" wedding saying.

Some girls paint their nails with polish in the team colors. One team even persuaded the boys to put polish on just their pinkie fingernails for luck in the boys' game. Wearing green when there is a ballgame on St. Patrick's Day is required.

Shamrock stickers on shoes or painted ones on faces could always be found that day – sometimes the holiday falls on Alaska state tourney week, as well. That just adds power to the luck of the Irish.

For Alaska teams, the road trip begins after the plane lands. Teams are on the road for as long as ten days before driving back to the airport. There are specific road trip procedures to ensure a win of the next game: when the van crosses railroad tracks, everyone must raise their feet; in a tunnel or going under an overpass, all must hold their breath; and everyone must scream "Slug Bug (plus its color)" when a VW Beetle is sighted.

Specific basketball pre-game routines include wearing the same street clothes, sitting in the same seat on the plane or bus, and eating the same meals as on the day the team last won a game. Something about the familiar is calming. So is music. Some athletes have a song or a soundtrack that inspires them, and they listen before every game. My teams usually chose a song for the season and played it over and over. I was secretly glad when the season of "Who Let the Dogs Out?" was over, but I never complained because the team thought it was perfect. We were undefeated that year.

As I ran errands and visited around town just before the Barrow team I coached was going to the state tournament, I grabbed the hand of every former Lady Whaler that I knew for luck. It felt good to connect with all those women, to join our hands and link our dreams. We didn't bring home the first place trophy but the women of three generations were cheering for us.

The choice of numbers on a uniform has its own bit of fancy. Some players want a number that relates to their life, like a birth date, age, the number dad wore, the number their boy/girl friend wears or that of a certain pro. Small players like to be number one. Daring players want thirteen. Some coaches don't even order a thirteen. Might be unlucky.

I had a player once who believed it was taboo to ever speak about injuries because saying the words would bring them upon us. We tried to honor her belief by playing charades to identify sore body parts instead of discussing the ailment out loud. Tiffany, in Larry Coulton's book, <u>Counting Coup</u>, always put on her uniform in the same order: shorts, shirt, right foot sock, left foot sock, right foot shoe, and then left foot shoe. She also sprinkled a pinch of sage into her shoes.

During the game, players develop mini-rituals in different game situations. At the free throw line, one player bounces the ball twice to a mental beat, then shoots the ball on the third beat. He does it every time. Another technique is to rub the bottom of both shoes before shooting or to wipe one shoe on the sock of the other leg. In the days of wooden floors, players would line up their feet at the nail in the center of the line. That went away with rubber and inlaid gym flooring. I must rotate the ball until the brand name is right side up before shooting a free throw. A former player bounced the ball once, then spun it in her hand, then shot.

The player taking out the ball might wipe her hand on her pants every single time or turn the ball so the lines are horizontal or refuse to look at the ball. In the last 33 years, one veteran coach waited to leave a gym where he was coaching or playing until his last shot went in. I have seen players who tarried on the court when it was time for the pre-game talk until they made a shot, or three in a row, or whatever they felt was needed to appease the gods of good luck. In basketball, jewelry cannot be worn, so heirloom earrings, St. Christopher's medals and talismans are not visible. I had a player who sewed a lucky charm onto the hem of her jersey and tucked it in out of sight. An excellent high school player kept a penny dated the year of his dad's birth in his shoe to feel like his dad was with him during the game. Martina Leavitt, one of Barrow's best ball players, used to keep a penny in her shoe "so she'd never be broke." Whatever the habit, it is done exactly the same every time.

Huddles in a game have their own ceremony. At the end, players either touch closed fists or stack open palms on one another and push them downward on a word. "Teamwork," "hustle," "kiita" (an Inupiaq word for let's go), and "defense" are all positive words to use. My middle school intramural players used "aggressiveness" and "conquer" to break the huddle. Their English teacher would have been proud. When I first arrived on the North Slope, I said "kiita" with my team and I knew it was a non-English word, so when we started saying "kikis," I thought that was another Inupiaq word. It wasn't – I had been screaming "kick ass" and didn't even know it.

The Barrow boys team have a game ending ceremony, after the shaking of hands with the opposing players, in which they perform some physical act as many times as they have won games during the year. For instance, all the boys will do ten

push-ups together if they have won ten games. The coach feels that it brings good karma.

Fans create their rites, too. Many wear team colors on game day, even if they are listening to the radio coverage at home. One loyal fan must have the kitchen clean and the living room vacuumed before she can listen to the game.

I've heard coaches of girls say that if their players' hair looks extra nice for a game, they will likely play well. When I asked for an explanation, I was told that the logic was that if they had spent hours braiding and styling hair, they were probably not stressed and would be relaxed and in the zone.

Probably, this logic justifies the value of all superstitions. Belief in the intangible helps keep a player relaxed, something necessary to make good split-second decisions in a game.

My favorite (and most effective) coaching superstition worked with a middle school team who lacked confidence. I wore a beige polyester tunic top trimmed with black stitching when we won our first game. After that, every time I wore that shirt, we won. Sometimes I told them that it had to be washed and I wore something else. Then, we usually lost. The girls were convinced that somehow that shirt had supernatural powers. I don't think they suspected that I only wore the shirt at games which I was positive that we were going to win. The magic spell

was cast. As the season progressed, I wore it more and more. The team was unstoppable by tournament time.

Whether athletes live in the jungles of Ecuador or on Alaska's tundra, they often find something to believe in, something outside them, something illogical, even mystical, to improve their chances of winning. Perhaps it is enough to simply have something in which to believe. Maybe, as Tennessee Williams quipped, "Luck is believing you are lucky."

*Coaching Tip*
*Prepare with hard work, but don't discount*
*the whimsy that the human spirit needs.*

# The Night the Ancients Danced

The Tetlin Wildlife Refuge Visitor Center had just opened for the summer season the day my husband and I stopped for a stretch break. It was mid-May and we were driving a remote section of the Alaska Highway en route from Anchorage to West Virginia.

Two Athabascan women monitored the immaculate log building. Their eyes lit up as we entered the main room, signed the visitor log, and looked at the nature displays all the while breathing freshly cut wood and sweet wood smoke. They greeted us with a smile, laying aside beadwork and a skin-sewing project, needles dangling. Their hands had been busy during the hours between visitors. We chatted about the weather and mentioned that we were from Barrow.

One of the ladies excitedly told us she had a house guest from Barrow, a mutual friend, Janelle Patkotak, and we talked more. Then they remarked that they were both from Northway.

I gasped, "Northway? I took a team there several years ago to play basketball."

One lady spoke up, "If it was a game played in Northway, I was in the bleachers." She paused and pointed to her co-worker, "And so was she!"

And the memories of that trip roared back.

As the girls' basketball coach and athletic director at Hopson Middle School in Barrow, I had been given the task to organize a one-week trip for the middle school basketball teams. It was important to maximize the $20,000 needed for airline tickets with as many games as could be scheduled.

Fairbanks was the closest city on a road system so we planned to fly there and play schools in town then drive to as many smaller towns that we could. Games were to be played in Healy, Tok, and Nenana, longtime opponents and gracious host schools. I examined a map to find other villages nearby and saw

tiny Northway. They had a school and it did have a middle school basketball program. I called. They were happy to provide accommodations for our boys and girls and schedule a middle school double header on the second Friday night in November.

The trip began in Fairbanks. We played Monroe Catholic School and showered there, then slept in a church and began the five hour drive to Tok the next morning. I drove the fifteen passenger van  with the girls' team and Gene Smith drove the boys' van.

Gene was a good friend, a wonderful PE aide for my HMS class, and he had a son on the team. He hailed from Los Angeles, and looked like a six-foot Michael Jordan with the same shaved head and ever present charismatic smile. Gene was also a US Army veteran. Smart, laid-back, wise in the ways of students, and fearless, he was an ideal chaperone for this trip.

The drive to Tok was memorable for the abundance of wildlife – moose, deer, a fox and a bear – and for the great food and hospitality at Fast Eddy's Restaurant. The logo for the place is a skinny man with a pizza running from a bear. Cheeseburgers and milkshakes for 20 adolescents, each ordered separately, had to have been as much a nightmare for the waitresses as it was delightful for the 20 students. Afterwards, the steady snow slowed us on the narrow, winding road as warm, full players slept in the van the last hour of the trip.

At the end of the short winter day, darkness fell quickly. The van headlights danced through bare tree trunks and branches as we shimmied and slid down the mountain to find Northway. Not one vehicle met us during the miles between the main road and the small town. When the two vans finally pulled into the school parking lot, I unpeeled my fingers from their death grip on the steering wheel and managed to laugh at Gene whose eyes were still wide with anxiety in the driver's seat of the boys' van. Sleepy kids were lugging their gear out of the van through the snow to the locker room. The small gym was rocking and rolling with a packed house of hometown fans. It was game time!

The first game pitted the Barrow boys against the young men from Northway. The members of both teams were small and scrappy. Long passes and terrific three-point shooting kept the crowd in an uproar. There were screams of delight for the home team and grudging applause when the guests played well. It was kind of the home team fans to cheer for us at all since our cheering section that night consisted of the girls team when the boys played and vice versa.

The game was close but we managed to pull ahead at the end to barely win. One of our boys, EJ, twisted his ankle during the game. We put ice on it and when I asked about medical services, the Northway principal explained that it would be easier to wait until morning and take him out by van, as a helicopter couldn't get in there during the snow storm.

That was one of my first realizations that playing ball in bush Alaska was unlike other places. We were isolated beyond anything I had ever experienced. In this case, we were on our own for medical care. Thank goodness, EJ's pain eased within the hour and he gingerly limped forward to shake hands after the game.

When the girls took the court for the second game, the noise became deafening. The coach had a daughter who was the star and seemed to be the only non-Native player in the game. The Northway girls seemed well-loved as everyone in the stands stood and cheered for every play they attempted. The volume went up when they scored.

I think we got beat that night. I remember that the coach's daughter played very well and that there were no incidents of poor sportsmanship or home cooking with the referees, just good basketball in a small, loud gym. I know I felt good about our effort but was exhausted from the long snowy drive in the dark.

After all the fans went home and the custodian picked up the trash in the bleachers and swept the gym floor and hallway, we were alone to shower, to shoot around, and to get ready for "bed" which was the usual air mattress and a sleeping bag in the classroom floor. The school cooks had left bag suppers in the cafeteria and we nibbled at sandwiches as we unwound from the evening's events.

My strongest memories of that night are not from the game but from the hours after the kids and coaches and chaperones were asleep. I was tired, almost at the point of being too tired to sleep. I rolled back and forth in my sleeping bag, readjusting the

mat under me, counting sheep, unsuccessfully trying to fall asleep. After a while, I gave up and stared at the classroom ceiling through the darkness.

Then I heard a pounding. First, I thought maybe it was my heart beat in the quiet but it was a different cadence, irregular, yet a pattern of vibrations. I thought students had come back into the school but I consulted my luminous dial watch and it was midnight. The band wouldn't be practicing in the middle of the night! I pulled the window shades to one side and peeked out. Nothing but darkness. I crawled back into my sleeping bag. The pounding grew stronger and seemed to be only in my head. It didn't hurt, but I tried to escape the pounding by tossing and turning, even by humming softly.

As minutes of sleeplessness grew into hours, the night grew darker and I thought I could see what resembled black ink spreading in the air of the classroom, forming large shapes at the same time the noise in my head morphed into chanting. Then, like the focus of an automatic camera lens, the shapes became clearer. Dark human silhouettes were moving with the beat. Paralyzed with fear, I tried to persuade myself that it was not a vision, that it was nothing but a simple dream. I forced one eye to open a tiny bit, just a slit, and could sense the desks in the room and the girls sleeping around me.

Still they danced, slower and less threateningly as time went on. I could see the faces of beautiful ancient men and women and perfect animals, wolves, bears, and wolverines, on the heads of dancers. I recognized the feeling I had had as a baby when someone was telling me a story but I couldn't understand the words. Then and now I tried to figure out the meaning from voice tone and motions. The dancers were telling me a story ... and I could not get it. Their meaning was strong and important and finally filled me with contentment and I slept as though I had been drugged.

When I awakened early the next morning, the girls were scurrying around, packing and making their usual trip after trip to the bathroom. Several teased me about "sleeping in." It was the only time I wasn't the first one awake on a trip in all my years traveling with students.

I don't know what happened that night. I talked to Gene who had no such experience in the next room and looked at me oddly when I described my night. Maybe I was tired to the point of hallucination. Maybe the bag supper contained food that disagreed with my digestion and gave me strange dreams. I

don't think so. I think of it as the night the ancients danced in my head. I have to believe that native culture, so foreign to many who have relocated to Alaska, found a way inside my semi-consciousness that night.

I've never been back to Northway, but every now and then, when the memory surfaces, I embrace it.

*Coaching Tip*
*Cherish the unexplainable.*

# Basketball as an Art Form

Even though not all participants in life are artists, we all notice moments of beauty. My observations lead me to believe that every human movement done well is beautiful, a form of art. Whether it is a figure skater's smoothly performed routine, a child pumping a soaring playground swing, or the wind-up of a collegiate softball pitcher, the action catches and pleases the human eye. Plus, it looks easy! Excellence often appears effortless, especially to less talented spectators. Great singers open their mouths and readily release heavenly sounds. The third grade classroom of a master teacher flows seamlessly through nine subjects every day. An expert mechanic diagnoses and repairs a screaming car engine in seconds. Most of us, however, know just enough to be dumbfounded at these skills.

Training, effort, and talent hide the complexities of astounding accomplishments from mere mortals who are only present to see the final outcome. As onlookers, we don't see the years spent preparing for the moments that seem simply perfect to us. Practice and attitude are vital to most achievements. Distinctive skill in basketball requires an investment in time generally proportional to the perception of ease by spectators. Coaches know that players destined for greatness have dues to pay: open-mindedness about learning and years of training, until their body reacts with little thought. The results of dedication offer one facet of the game to all, players and spectators – the incredible beauty of basketball played well. The physical beauty of basketball takes many forms. The grace of a runner, the strength of a jumper, the measured motion of a human chess game of offenses and defenses all contribute to this sport.

The effortlessness of first-rate basketball reminds me of professional ballroom dancing. Opposing players become dance partners with synchronized movements, mirroring each other. There is smoothness in the steps, yet the tension of partnership in both. On the dance floor, the man usually leads. He leans and presses one way or the other to subtly guide his partner to move with him in the same direction. She responds, gazes into his eyes, and changes position to compliment his. His hand presses in the middle of her back as she tilts backward, trusting his strength, arching her spine and extending her arms over her head, pausing to create a picturesque human form. Likewise, the motions of athletes in a basketball game create the same statue inspiring forms.

In basketball, the offensive player with the ball leads the movements, with the goal of eluding the defensive player. The defender does not gaze into the eyes of the opponent, however. I always taught players to watch the belly button area of those they guarded. Eyes can mislead, but the tummy must go with the trickiest of moves. In a regional play-off in which Princess, a tiny high school point guard, ponytail bobbing as she dribbled, lunged her head and body forward repeatedly trying to advance the ball. Instinctively, almost effortlessly, the body of Bethel's little guard, Cindy, responded in the exact opposite direction, thwarting her forward progress. Cindy reflected the jabbing footwork, the head fakes, and the changes of speed until Princess gathered muscles and tendons to push past her and stretch full length to shoot a lay-up. The movement and the total focus amazed; her effort created a shape that inspired younger players to emulate her and those with an artist's sensitivity to smile.

Away from the ball, inside players struggle; the offensive player moves constantly to free up space to allow reception of a pass. The defender uses a repertoire of steps and arm movements to stay in the space between the ball and the opposing player.

In her last home game, Barrow senior center Bernice Oyagak, and her opponent, tall, blonde Kirsten from Nome, nicknamed "Polar Bear," extended their lanky teenaged figures with all arms reaching and all legs stretched to establish position inside. It was hard to look away from their footwork and ballet-like upper body movements at both ends of the court. When a pass was completed, the defender immediately changed her stance to discourage, even block, the shot. The interaction, which could have looked like a wrestling match between less skilled players, instead appeared graceful.

Well-toned physiques are obvious in both sports. Bright uniforms made of shimmering dazzle cloth barely touch the

athletes' bodies. The fabric skims over muscular shoulders and backsides to outline the human figure. Bare arms and legs are exposed, creating some of the same effects as a competitive dancer's slinky formal gown, clinging here and there but rippling like silk when leg muscles move. Both outfits cover extensively yet flow as the form changes shape.

Powerful legs, delicate hand movements, whispered words between partners, foreheads shining with sweat are all commonalities of the gym and the ballroom. So is the importance of focus. The score in both sports depends on focus and clarity of movement. One misstep or lapse in judgment can determine the outcome. A stumble by a professional dancer can ruin the chances of a high score, and so can a missed free throw shot in a basketball game. A lack of anticipation on the court may allow the other team to steal the ball; on the dance floor one partner may miss a cue that ruins a performance.

Multiply the grace of one pair of partners by five and interweave their motions for full-court choreography. Participants' uncanny awareness of their own body, of the defense, their teammates, and the goal expands the dance. The ball moves like a needle through fabric, finding a receiver with the passer not even looking in that direction. A screen is set and the targeted defender does a 360 degree roll to avoid it and continue on her path. Well executed plays baffle teams who have spent less time practicing. Conversely, good defensive teams force offensive plays to be repeated, turning the level of play up a notch. Shuffles and spins, stops and starts, dodges and feints, and just enough contact to remain legal builds a crescendo that ends only with a goal scored or a change of possession. Then the dance begins anew, a different partner in the lead.

When the dance on the basketball court approaches perfection, players and spectators feel the "click," the "game on," the "force." High school teams don't generally play entire games with excellence, but there are short periods of time that approach it. I coached a great high school girls' team during such a time during the last seconds of a holiday tournament championship at Skyview High School in Soldotna, Alaska. The Barrow girls were playing Nikiski. A shot by Nikiski with five seconds left tied the score. We called a timeout and would inbound the ball under Nikiski's goal. My plan was for us to hold the ball and hang on for the overtime but before I could speak, senior forward Bekah Gueco proposed that she throw the ball to a player at half court who would throw it to a player waiting under our goal that would shoot it and win the game. This simple plan used skills that had been drilled every practice of their lives. I deferred to the absolute confidence of the team, just reminded them whatever else they did, they must keep the ball out of the other team's hands.

Some players say that their perception changes when everything falls into place, that all movements slow down and they can anticipate and perform better. I felt that the last five seconds of that game lasted a full minute. The other team was tired and fell for Bekah's faked in-bounds pass. She threw it the other direction to Julieanna waiting at half court. Julieanna used every fiber of strength in her wiry sophomore body to throw a perfect baseball pass to waiting Ashley who shot the short jump shot she had practiced a zillion times. It went in. Fans stood to watch with a heart-pounding, open-mouthed paralysis. A game played at the highest level of skill is dream-like. Skill and strength and endurance meld together into something splendid. Competition provides its own scale of success. There are the points scored and the opponents bested, but there are larger effects from the pure joy of performing well. After the pain of losing or the joy of winning such a match subsides, the memory of excelling and being part of the beauty lingers in the participant's mind.

Even though most members of the audience are not likely to create a statue or a painting of the action, the impression of loveliness remains with them as well. Often fans say, "Wow, that was a good game!" when they mean, "How beautifully the game was played tonight!"

*Coaching Tip*
*Practice provides the basis*
*for the beauty of basketball.*

# School Politics:
# Never Cut the Secretary's Daughter

I learned this concept the hard way. My excuse is that Buffy, the school secretary's tenth grade daughter, could not play ball. She could not even dribble the length of the court. Buffy giggled a lot. She was a cute kid, smart enough to get by without doing too much, and badly spoiled. She had everything money could buy from high fashion clothes beginning in first grade to a new truck when she turned sixteen. However, she had redeeming qualities – she was perky and generous and popular with her peers. I liked her, too, but she had no basketball skills. More importantly, she was not willing to work to obtain skills. Buffy wanted to wear a shiny uniform and run onto the court in the spotlight. She did not want to put in hours building strength and endurance or learning to handle a basketball. The varsity team had been so weak the year before that she was included as a freshman when there were vacancies in the travel roster. The former coach, also a teacher at the school, understood who buttered his bread. I did not.

I went to the front office to give Lula, the secretary, the official roster of players after the cut was finalized. I spoke to her privately and explained that daughter Buffy did not have varsity level skills yet. Buffy wasn't completely off the team; she had made the junior varsity program. With playing experience gained this year, I felt that she could earn a spot on the varsity team next year, as an eleventh grader. As the air in the office became frosty, I realized that her family's high expectations did not include participation on the junior varsity squad, but I had certainly underestimated their disappointment.

Lula's big eyes were filled with tears when I broke the bad news, but I mistakenly believed that she understood. Later, I learned that within a few minutes of my visit, she fell into the principal's arms, alternately swinging her shoulder length

braids, sobbing, shrieking, and begging that he fire me. He called me to the office to discuss the decision. I invited him to look at the point system I had devised for tryouts. According to the rubric, even leaving her on the JV squad was a stretch. "Come to practice and see for yourself," I begged. He shook his head and sighed, no doubt knowing what lay ahead for me. To this day, I know that I was right in my assessment. I just didn't know how hard it would be to stick to my guns.

Lula was a Samoan female warrior. She fought mightily for all her children and nieces and nephews and was rarely crossed. She and her family members were physically large; usually children in her family could locate items on the top of the refrigerator before they finished elementary school. They were also infamous for getting their way. Those in the court system were familiar with their methods. I wish someone had told me.

Since this was my first year as the varsity coach at this particular high school, I didn't realize the power of the secretary. She made the travel arrangements for the team, turned in documentation for paychecks, handled all orders, communicated with parents, and generally had the power to ruin my life.

My first clue was the school public address system announcement broadcasting the change of the girls' basketball practice time to 6 AM. We had been practicing at 6 PM, but it seemed that other uses of the gym had come up. Yep, the secretary also handled gym use schedules. We practiced at that ungodly hour for a week before the "typo" was corrected.

Then, the season began and we traveled to the first away game with the boys' team. We all arrived at the budget hotel together. The boys had reservations for four double rooms. We had NO reservations but mercifully, there was a suite empty and we piled twelve players and a coach in two beds, a pullout couch, and a whirlpool tub. Some girls had backaches; others had stiff necks on game day.

After the fiasco in the hotel, parents called the school to express their outrage about the sleeping arrangements. Lula explained that there had been a misunderstanding, that I was new and didn't understand how to check in to a hotel. Years later, I also learned that she whispered that she had heard that I wanted to sleep with the girls. I didn't know this murmur at the time because many of the parents of the players had known me for many years and didn't want to embarrass me with the ridiculous rumors Lula was spreading.

Then, there were flight arrangements. We traveled to remote areas of Alaska to play ball, places that did not have road access. So we flew, either by commercial jet on Alaska Airlines, or by small airlines like Frontier or Hageland Air. Small planes were chartered when special circumstances existed. When we went to Nome, the girls and I flew three hours to Anchorage, sat six hours, and then caught a flight back up to Nome, another three-hour flight. It was a long day, twelve hours of travel. The boys had been provided a charter flight, total travel time, two hours and fifteen minutes. I complained to the principal. He shrugged and told me to discuss it with Lula. Evidently, coaches are not the only ones who need to cater to secretaries.

When we traveled to Sitka, only one van was rented and we were supposed to alternate use of it between the girls and boys team. Seemingly, that was not communicated clearly enough to the boys' coaches. As the girls walked up and down the hill to eat at McDonalds, the Sitka principal took pity on us and let me drive his school's vehicle for the weekend.

The boys sported new warm-up uniforms, travel sweats, personalized shooter shirts and windbreakers, blue and gold basketball shoes, and duffle bags with shiny embroidered numbers that matched their jerseys. Donations had come in to finance these extras. The girls got sweat suits near mid-season. They had held fund-raisers to earn them. Our order was so late arriving that I called the company. The order had never been placed, must've been a malfunctioning fax machine.

There were other inequities. Invitations to dinner from community groups for the girls' team were mislaid. So many purchase orders disappeared that I started placing orders for necessary items such as awards using my credit card and had them sent to my home address in order to assure delivery. Lula forgot to inform the girls or me when travel plans changed. The phone from the girls coaching office was requisitioned for another area of the school. Ditto the furniture from the girls' coaches' office. By the time I got my check for the year, I had almost forgotten it was a paid position. Problems with paperwork in the front office delayed payment for several months.

The telephoned death threats were actually pretty funny. What killer is going to leave a message on an answering machine telling the victim that she would be murdered in the center of the court at halftime during the homecoming festivities? We had caller ID so it was clear where the threat originated. I chose to ignore it. Besides, a bullet proof vest would destroy the line of my formal dress. I did think of the threat as I was escorted to the homecoming queen's court and hoped that if I was going to die, it would be before I had to walk another step in high heels.

I came the closest to giving up on a rainy night after an away game. For some reason, probably to antagonize me, Lula had traveled with both teams to a distant town. The boys were playing at 6:30 and the girls were playing at 8:00. All restaurants in town closed at 9:00 PM. The girls' game would not be over before the restaurants closed for the night. Teenagers, boys or girls, eat a lot after a game. Thinking ahead, the girls and I ordered several large pizzas and salad and soda from a nearby pizzeria, paid for them, and arranged early delivery to the hotel so we would have late night food. We looked forward to a pizza feast in our rooms following the game. When we arrived, tired and hungry, the boys' team and coaches plus Lula were sitting in the lobby finishing up the crumbs of our dinner. I demanded payment. Lula rotated her face in a circle and gave me attitude about how the town enjoyed the boys' game so much that they treated them to pizza. The girls and I loaded back into the rental van and found an all night grocery store and made subs at midnight. I was reimbursed for the pizza weeks later.

I tried to rationalize all the mayhem. Maybe these things would have happened anyway. Plagues do occur. Locusts do descend from the heavens. Boils and blisters inflict pain. Groups of people are persecuted for no reason. However, I am not a martyr. I've decided that sleeping and eating weigh in just a hair above integrity. If a secretary's kid ever again wants to play on my team, I'll find her a uniform!

*Coaching Tip*
*Do not ever cut the high school secretary's daughter
from the varsity team.*

# Ice Cream Classic

Alaskan villages, from Barrow's Beaufort Sea ice pack to the wildlife of Seward's Resurrection Bay, from Kotzebue and its inevitable spring blizzard to the glaciers of Sitka, prevail as spectacular locations on the planet. Traveling with a team to compete in Alaska provides experiences that rival National Geographic layouts for beauty and unique cultures. My favorite visit with a team has always been to a village in the interior of the state called Nenana.

South from Fairbanks, the Parks Highway winds gently up and down mountains, cutting paths through pristine forests until an odd looking white tripod fifteen feet tall comes into view along the road. It stands at the paved cutoff on the left. The tripod marks the point where the main street of Nenana intersects the highway. This is the first noticeable human settlement of any size (population 402) on the road south.

The little town of Nenana is a stone's throw from the Tanana River where the Yutana Barge Lines originate. The long arched highway bridge is an eye-catching work of art over the river. For years, barges from Nenana have carried supplies to the all the towns on the Yukon River. The Alaska Railroad once ran right through town.

The historic character of the town, which was once the center of transportation in interior Alaska, radiates from the log cabin businesses, the museum which was once the train station, and the quaint main street. Tourism must be a summertime business because there are photo opportunities with painted plywood backgrounds tucked into alleys near the main street. The girls pulled them out and took pictures of each other in a fake Nenana jail cell to send home.

There must be summer festivals, as well, because "River Daze" titles are prominent on the wooden sets. If you squint a bit, you can imagine river and train visitors of the past trudging up from the river or across the street from the train station to

the Moocher's Bar (which really does exist) on the right side of the street. In the fall, yellow willow leaves rustle in the wind and the smell of drying smoked salmon permeates the air so strongly that it can be tasted.

Each year since 1917, Nenana has hosted the Nenana Ice Classic, an unusual event. When the river freezes over in the fall, a huge tripod (like the one at the entrance to town) is placed two feet deep in the ice. It is connected to a digital clock which stops precisely when the ice breaks. All winter, risk-takers have spent $5 per ticket to guess the time and date that the ice will break up. Tickets are on sale state-wide and most folks buy more than one. The winner earns a percentage of the proceeds. Over $10 million has been distributed since the event began. The highest jackpot to date was in 2000 when the jackpot was $335,000. A non-profit organization manages the proceeds to support the Nenana library, school, senior center, visitor center and to fund scholarships.

With a clever twist of the event's name, a creative athletic director at the school began an Ice Cream Classic Basketball Tournament held in early November every year. Middle school teams appear from all over the state, sleep in classrooms, eat in the school cafeteria, and play ball for three glorious days. The teams attending pay an entrance fee; they buy meal tickets and inundate the grocery store and souvenir shops causing the local economy to flourish somewhat during that weekend. Our teams also took part in side trips to Mt. McKinley (Denali) to drive through the park. We'd usually see moose and if there was enough snow, we always had a girls versus boys snowball battle at some point in the road trip. In November, sometimes there are roads closed because of too much snow, but the stunning park amazes viewers from any vantage point, during any season, even middle-schoolers who live in the arctic. The feeling of being surrounding by huge mountains, their sharp white edges against the clear blue Alaskan sky is mesmerizing. Even

North Carolina blue has some competition from the color of the sky over the 49<sup>th</sup> state.

Another remarkable part of the tournament was the absence of trophies. The winning teams are served ice cream after every victory. And the best part, the years that we won games, there was always enough extra ice cream so that the winning players could invite the losing team members to share in the spoils. Development of friendships with kids from other remote places was a natural event, cultivated by supervised social events such as dances and dinners that allowed students to interact off the court.

The people of Nenana welcome the young ballplayers with open arms. Students are allowed inside smoke houses to see the process of drying and smoking salmon strips, fish wheels are explained, and stores and museums are willing to open at any hour to accommodate the basketball schedule. The culture is somewhat different from that of other native Alaskans. The inland community subsistence activities are not at all the same as coastal ones. My Inupiat students from Barrow understood whaling and ice cellars but were amazed at the fall salmon processing and the motion of the gigantic fish wheels. They were also enthralled with the welcome they received. Everyone was friendly, even during fiercely played basketball games.

However, one year I had a problem. Piggy, a sixth grader, was having a birthday during the tournament, on November 5. I hadn't had the foresight to buy gifts and a cake as we came through Fairbanks, so her birthday party presented some difficulty.

Back on the main highway (then down a cutback to the older Parks Highway) stands a building made of huge logs, a restaurant/bar called The Monderosa, famous for burgers and now memorable to my middle school basketball team as the setting of a party.

In a town with no bakery, no ice cream shop, and the Monderosa as the only eating establishment, I was hard pressed to host an appropriately gala event. We rounded up two frozen Sara Lee chocolate cakes and the last box of birthday candles at the only grocery store and loaded up the van with twelve girls. We piled into the Monderosa in midafternoon, hoping to avoid possible serious drinkers of the evening. Enthusiastic waitresses let me in the kitchen to arrange both cakes (now thawed) on a tray, and helped smooth the icing so they appeared to be one cake and poke twelve pink candles into the top. Amid the haze of cigarette smoke and the smell of beer, we had a kid's birthday party. The bar occupants were as jubilant as the girls and joined us in singing "Happy Birthday" to Piggy more than once. I know there would have been free rounds of drinks had the guests of honor been a decade or so older.

Only in Alaska.

*Coaching Tip*
*Trips can be winners, too.*

# Electronics

I knew at an early age I had the gift of nosiness. My family was on a party line when I was a child – our telephone was on a network with several other families. Any member of every family on the party line could listen in on every other conversation and I was quite sure that our neighbors knew some of the content of my chats because I could hear them breathing as they listened in. If I picked up the receiver during a call already in progress, I was supposed to say "Excuse me," and replace the handset. I didn't always do what I was supposed to do because I wanted to pay back those who may have listened in on me, oh, and let's face it, I wanted to get the scoop. I also hated to go to bed as a child because I was afraid I would miss something.

As an adult I learned that good coaches have this common aptitude: they are nosy. When "nosiness" seems more in good taste than bad (and that line is a fine one), we rename it "curiosity." Curiosity gains information which fuels the power of dealing with people, especially the delicate machinery of young people and competitive sports.

As the world of electronics rushes into the twenty-first century, nosiness is not only permitted, it is enhanced by tools that didn't exist even twenty years ago. When I returned to coaching, I was agape and agog at the capability for finding out stuff.

Picture this, our sunny breakfast nook of 1990, converted into a basketball "War Room" from November to March each year. Shelves were stuffed with play manuals, coaching "Bibles," books written by coaches, about players, videos, and notebooks of statistics. A calendar of the five month season took center stage, then charts of players, the philosophy of the season, inspirational quotes, scouting information, newspaper clippings, photos of team members, and lists – lots of lists: phone numbers, team rosters, junior varsity rosters, players to watch at the middle school or elementary level. White clipboards with markers hung on hooks. Stacks of pamphlets with contact information for various areas of health and well-being cluttered the shelves. I gloried in the amount of paraphernalia and the space it consumed. Sometimes when I couldn't sleep, I'd slip out of the bed and sit at the table with a mug of warm cocoa and bask in the nook's surroundings. I thought I had all the information imaginable in order to coach.

My imagination was obviously limited. I would not have believed that all those records, in 2005, could be a click away on a laptop computer, that my students would have their own tiny cell phones in their pockets, the vehicles would have a GPS on the dash and that the quality of basketball would improve with the gadgetry of modern electronics. Is someone hurt? Is the team van driver lost? Whip out a phone and find out if a parent can come, if this injury is serious, or where we turn to find the gym. The nosiness monster grew inside me and the breakfast nook lost its clout.

The season calendar was easily transferred to a computerized version on which notes could be added. The smelly magic marker needed to make notes on the wall calendar was an odor of the past.

Folders on my desktop were labeled "Offensive Plays" and "Defenses." Offensive and defensive plays for any situation or any combination of players are obtainable online, even with animation. No longer are felt tip marked Xs and Os and clipboards necessary – a computer screen is all that is needed to introduce a new play. I filed "Stats" by team and by individual players, "Rosters" of our team together with every team we played, and "Contact Info" for coaches and players. Lists of links of newspaper coverage of us and our opponents, complete with scoring data were at my fingertips, free of newsprint smudges, thank you very much.

My books became dusty – I could google an author and a basketball concept much quicker than I could find it in a book in print. Videos were useful for specific games or players, but it was easier to burn a section of the video to a DVD to use at team sessions on a laptop.

Coaches have always wanted to know what their team members were thinking. If only we could see into their minds. That dream came true for me. I learned exactly what my players thought of practices, games, and me. All I had to do was click on

MySpace, Facebook, or Bebo account photos and read the players' reactions and thoughts. Anyone could! It wasn't always pleasant or predictable, but an unavoidable strength of teenagers is that they communicate with each other very frequently. Public journals and blogs shared more personal information. The adage "Be careful what you wish for" occurred to me.

That still wasn't enough. I wanted to know what other coaches and fans thought. I could find out on websites devoted to the commentary of fans of high school sports – in Alaska, one site is *AlaskaPreps.com.* Opinions on all things related to high school hoops abound. The facts are available, too. The website for the governing body of all secondary school activities in Alaska, *asaa.org,* is available 24 hours a day. Find out who won, who scored, and what the new rules are.

Social issues are not secrets any more. Any computer user can ask questions about health concerns of live medical personnel that are often difficult for young women to discuss: depression, sexually transmitted diseases, pregnancy, even suicide are addressed online. We can all view all our hometown sex offenders, complete with picture and address, from the on-line listings. The trial and hearing calendar is available in every town in Alaska with a court room. Treatment facilities have websites with pertinent information. Counseling hotlines await our questions. Good informational sites for youngsters give tips for conditioning and training. Who knows – perhaps the future holds computer software to replace coaches and parents!

Fifty years ago, the score of a basketball game was updated with a dusty rag and a piece of chalk on a blackboard as baskets were made. Last week I watched the state tournament championship game being played a thousand miles away on television as the score book stats, shot chart, and percentages for the participants streamed onto my laptop screen. Mind-boggling.

I guess I could take a picture of the warm, cozy breakfast nook and use it as a screen saver to enjoy as I drink my cocoa, but there is no need. The use of technology has fulfilled my curiosity beyond my wildest dreams and has done so with such efficiency that I now have time to be curious about other things. Is Ravi Shankar really Norah Jones' father? Does popcorn have

more calories than chips? Are badgers the same as wolverines? Gotta run, I have googling to do ...

*Coaching Tip*
*Electronics are your friends.*

# Differences in the Huddle

Once upon a time (before Title IX), American parents and coaches believed that the exertion of running from one end of the gym to the other would damage the frail internal organs of the women. Another belief was that female athletes would likely get breast cancer from bruising blows to their chests. "Girls are gonna get hurt … " echoed throughout the country. Never mind that most women of that time in Alaska hauled water, chopped wood, washed clothes by hand, cooked from scratch, and gave birth with limited medical personnel available.

As recently as the 1970s, basketball teams for girls consisted of six players – two could play in the back half of the court for defense, two could play in the front half of the court on offense, and two were rovers and were allowed to play the whole court.

It was recommended that all the girls wear padded undergarments to protect their tender upper bodies. After several years without death or serious injury to young women, the rules for girls' basketball were amended into practically the same ones used by the boys. Forty years later, regulations of boys and girls basketball are nearly identical. Minor differences include a smaller basketball and uniform specifications. Equity was mostly instituted. Oh, except for the perception that boys and girls would perform exactly the same in the game and in response to coaching – a dragon that needs slaying.

No matter that the rules are fair, there are far deeper influences on children's behaviors than the regulations of the

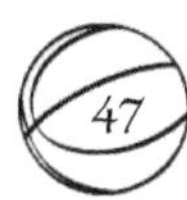

game, and some are connected to gender. The lasses and lads of the court are still different.

Except for stand-in appearances when a regular coach of a boys' team was late or needed a sub and my one season stint with a Little Dribblers elementary co-ed team, my experience has all been with girls. I had assumed that coaching was the same for both genders, and truly, there are more similarities than not, but there are glaring differences, both physiologically and psychologically. Watching and talking to coaches of boys' teams has provided intriguing general information about their players' behaviors.

Physically, there are clear differences between males and females. Research is ongoing on the subject of injuries due to anatomical differences. Girls appear to have more blown out knees, possibly because the angle of the muscular connection from hip to knee is different. Girls' hips are wider than boys which may cause a weaker knee ligament attachment. Jumping and spinning may put more stress on the female knee because of more weight in the hips. There seem to be more complaints about shin splints by girls and more knee pain. Estrogen levels may play a part in women's injuries, but there is much that is unknown about human anatomy. Whatever the cause, girls need to need to know about how their joints work and how to jump, land, and twist without damaging knees. Longer stretching sessions before a workout may be beneficial to girls. Finally, careful selection of supportive devices to protect knee ligaments is also important for female athletes.

Psychologically, there are more subtle differences and they are likely to change as society changes. Environment contributes to the expectations of girls and boys, and these are evolving, but distinctions between genders remain, even on the basketball court. Certainly, there are overlaps in behavior and no one general trait is true for all girls or all boys, but some particular general-related qualities have arisen, at least among my colleagues.

First, according to male coaches who have coached both genders, a team of boys is more likely to function without interference from personalities or off-court drama than a girls' team. For example, if Mary feels that her boyfriend has been taken by Sue, Sue will not EVER get the ball from Mary. Conversely, if Moe feels that Stan hurt him personally in some way, no matter how horribly, it will likely be put aside for the team to work together effectively. Moe will still pass the ball to

Stan when he is open. These coaches strongly suggest that girls need to resolve personal issues before taking the court. Parents who have raised both sons and daughters note that boys also seem to be more driven to win. This may help them to more easily shift personal issues to the back burner.

Again, coaches with experience with both genders agree that, for boys, winning seems to be the priority in basketball and that young men appear to have more innate confidence and are less concerned about mistakes they make. After missing a shot or a defensive assignment, boys forgive themselves faster than their female counterparts. After Joann misses three shots, she will probably quit shooting, even though she is a good shooter and can get open for a clear shot. She will need to be coached to continue taking the risk of shooting. After missing ten shots, Jack needs absolutely no encouragement to take the next open opportunity to fire the ball up.

I have observed that young men generally criticize their peers more quickly and callously than girls. A missed pass or a poor play by a teammate will more likely spark negative comments or smiles by the boys. Girls will more likely respond to bad play with "Hang in there" or offer specific ideas for improvement. They will certainly not scream with laughter when a teammate gets hit in the groin as the guys are apt to do.

Many girls maintain off-court manners while playing. Some apologize after physical impact on the court. Basketball is a contact sport, in spite of the rules, and some girls will whisper, "Sorry" or "Excuse me" when there is a collision with a set screen or when rebounding position is gained. Young women regularly attend to injured players during the game, extending a hand to help them up or running for ice or bandages when needed. Although boys also help fallen players, I observe it is less frequently. I have had girls actually thank me for the workout after every practice. No reports of similar behavior by boys were noted by their coaches.

Sometimes girls will hold back when they are playing against friends or weaker athletes. I have felt the same subliminal pull and have sensed myself retreat into a less physical game with weaker opponents. I've used this thinking as the rationale to invite talented male athletes to practice with the girls in a controlled setting. The girls play harder against them.

After a game, male players leave discussing the score and a few clear moments of glory. Girls leave the game knowing details – what everyone in the stands was wearing, who was sitting with whom, and the expressions on the faces of players when game events occurred. Girls recall all this in addition to the score and the highlighted moments of the competition.

I have noticed in discussions after the game, male coaches and players seem to be more prone to blame sources outside themselves for a loss – the referees, the schedule, the poor travel arrangements, the noise that kept them up the night before. Female coaches and players internalize the responsibility; they usually blame themselves. To restore healthy optimism requires a different style of coaching for each reaction.

It is not unfair to coach girls differently than boys and it is not a put-down. Both genders have strengths and weaknesses. It just makes sense to assess which coaching styles and strategies work for each individual player and use them to build a good team as well as healthy individuals. One place to start is the gender of the team.

And perhaps everyone can live happily ever after ...

*Coaching Tip*
*Match coaching style to the needs of players.*

# Band of Sisters

They file into the bleachers well before tip-off time in small gyms all over the state. They nimbly climb the set of stairs with arms full of diaper bags, snacks, and cushions for padding the hard spectator seats.

It seems that their bodies are softened by the years since high school as they laughingly stake their claim on an area of the bleachers and move efficiently to organize their family for the game. They lay babies in swaddling fur parkas between the benches with a guard child stationed near their head to ward off those who might inadvertently step on a sleeping infant. They arrange jackets shed by youngsters and husbands for a smiling nest of children who scamper back and forth to the concession stand for slushies and corn dogs and sweets. They seldom travel alone, but if they do, they quickly find a game buddy to sit beside, share popcorn, programs, and conversation all evening.

Finally, they settle in for the introduction of players, only to jump to their feet and yell and applaud for every son or daughter or niece or nephew or cousin or neighbor that is on the team. It doesn't matter what personal relationship they have with the players; it only matters that the team represents the small town where they all live. In years past, these women were the daughters who were applauded as they ran to the center circle before the game. Once they, too, were in bright uniforms facing strangers to play the sport that still brings them all together, basketball. They understand how important the fans are to the participants and they are there to remember and to relight their spirit and that of their village. They are loud and opinionated. Their camaraderie is stronger than a common race or religion or role in life. They are not all mothers, not all housewives or co-workers but they are all women who have faced the realities of adulthood. They live with zest and take pride in the people and place where they live. They are still enchanted by the romance of basketball. They are honest and open in their assessment of play. They act as if they know that life is fleeting and some hours of life are precious, like those at ballgames, and must be savored.

I joined this league of female warriors as our middle daughter played junior varsity basketball and we gathered at 4 PM every Friday and Saturday for four long jv and varsity games per evening. Even with my veteran ball-player husband sitting right by me, I leaned forward and strained backwards to hear opinions of the other women: "That girl needs to get more sleep at night and quit smoking" about a luckless, slow, shooter; or advice, "Tell your daughter if she gets back faster on defense, her friends will follow;" or questions tinged with resentment, "Why is that coach yelling at our team? They're okay." Mostly, though, they cheered. Anything. Players entering the game, players coming out of the game. Standing ovations for those who fouled out. Index finger jabbing cheers that identify the visitor who fouled our players, "YOU, YOU, YOU!" They lead the crowd on a whole different level than the school cheerleaders.

Parents were at every game, home and away, sporting matching blue and gold t-shirts, cheering for their sons and daughters. Lilly Nungasak, a former star and coach was there, too, laughing and noticing details in the play that others missed. Former players and their friends were there; the list goes on and on.

Some of the women of my time are gone now.

Jodie always sat on the top bench, a prime location because the wall is close enough to lean against. She brought her three children when they were all small and sat with her husband, Vic, among family members and friends. She smiled as she separated the rough-housing boys, and doled out baby bottles for the youngest. One of the boys bounced up and down the bleachers dozens of times per game while his older brother sat and watched intently. Jodie and Vic were high school sweethearts and both were outstanding athletes. They played city league basketball for years after graduation. I can't remember ever seeing Jodie miss a lay-up; her form was fundamentally perfect. Vic scored readily from outside, usually playing with a grin on his face. One morning Jodie didn't wake up and, a few months later, Vic crashed his four-wheeler. Both their funerals were in that gym.

Emma Booth always sat near the side rails, behind the home team's bench. Her loud voice did not match her tiny wiry body. She screamed constantly in support of the home team and her twin girls Mary and Marilyn, who both played varsity basketball. Emma never missed a home game. She cheerfully called attention to errors made by the referees against the home team. The fall after the girls graduated, I asked her who she was gonna cheer for now and she responded – "I'll always be there to yell for my Whalers!" It was the last time I ever spoke to her. She died in her sleep that winter.

Lauren Danner frolicked with her large family at mid-court across from the score table during games. As a college student who visited during breaks from school, she cheered with a cousin or younger brother or sister in her lap for other siblings or cousins or uncles who were playing or coaching. She played, too, in her day, with heart and without the tipukness (Inupiat for prissiness) generally associated with beautiful women. In my mind, I can see her long hair flying behind her as she spun a child around to amuse him. She did not live to tell her son about those days. They will do it when he is old enough.

As years go by they will be replaced by younger lovers of basketball who find time for renewal and companionship in the bleachers as women have done in the past, with a long Saturday night at the games. I was a long way from my extended family during my years in the bleachers and the women around me gave me strength. Their actions modeled love and loyalty and pride. No matter what had hurt me during the week or what worry my own daughters or students presented, I could face it, deal with it, and if need be, laugh it off, in the presence of the band of sisters and our common love of the home basketball game.

*Coaching Tip*
*Be aware of the culture in the bleachers.*

# Consider the Source

All coaches endure tons of unsolicited advice. Some advisors are motivated by their personal interest in your team. Fans, especially relatives of players, lead this list.

A limited number of folks advise with honest helpfulness. Count trusted family members and coaching colleagues in this tiny group. Some acquaintances, convinced of their superior athletic knowledge, want to forcefully impose their ideas. No discussion. They are simply right.

Relatives are the most emotional fans. They are on the sidelines, watching their little girls grow up, a difficult task all by itself. Also, these girls are competing and everyone who loves them wants them to be winners. Finally, the competition takes place in the world of sports. Dear ole dad and brother and uncle and gramps often think that they possess secret information about sports to pass along to their girl ... and to her coach. And with all this baggage, passionate family supporters sometimes become unreasonable and incoherent. They don't mean to be inappropriate; they just lose the ability to be clear-headed.

Uncle Joe shouts during the game for all to hear, especially the coach, "C'mon, she just needs time to warm up" after his kid is taken out of the game for losing the ball four straight times. Translation: I want her to succeed.

Dad roars, "Play the subs!" The team is only up by five points in the last quarter. Translation: I want my daughter to play.

Big brother screams, "Watch your passes!" This tidbit points, rather inaccurately, to the need for better throws. Translation: I want her to do well and wish someone would catch a pass she flings.

Grandpa preaches, "Work her hard, make her run." Translation: Please have high expectations for my granddaughter, we can't do a thing with her at home.

Dad hugs the coach and whispers with great emotion, "Coach her good." Translation: I don't have a clue what to do but I want my baby girl to do well.

You must smile and be polite but immediately delete all the wisdom offered by biased fans. Advice coming at you from fans and family is distracting and often pointless. I tell myself to be patient and to realize that the advice serves a purpose: therapy for those who cannot control much in their beloved teenager's life. But, the peanut gallery usually has an agenda and it is not necessarily the one promoting the team's best interest.

The best advice you are going to get will come from those in your life who understand the sport you coach and truly want to help you become better at your job. Consider yourself lucky if you have one of these in your life. I was blessed to have two, a husband, Roger, and a dear friend, Dennis Boddy. I disagreed with a lot of the advice they gave and left the room hundreds of times in the midst of "coaching the coach" sessions, but several brilliant ideas were worth all the bogus ones. Dennis showed me a full court press for a short, fast team that won ballgame after ballgame. Simply, you put the tallest girl on the squad on the ball and let the quickest players handle the backcourt and pick off long passes. Great idea! Roger explained to me time after time that you can't coach every quality needed for basketball success – heart for example, and height. When my fondness for a player blinded me to her slowness or attitude, Roger could see it and guide me to notice it. These kinds of reality checks help a coach focus and improve.

I want to be a good coach and leader; my priorities and goals solid and clear. For that reason, I am careful in accepting assistance. I strive to make and stand by my own decisions. This

kind of power extends beyond the athletic arena. When a female coach models independence and self-reliance, the lives of the watching young women are affected. The influence is felt in their family relationships to behavior with their boyfriends to their workplace, to merely doing their schoolwork. When the coach's strength is visible on the court or in the locker room to the next generation of women, the players, they see their own potential and the world shifts a little.

In my first job as a varsity high school basketball coach, the boys' coach, Randy Shafer, was well established. That's an understatement. More accurately, the community worshiped the slim, goateed man. He could do no wrong even though rumors of immoral behavior flitted like bats around him after every wild weekend. He sang the lyrics of his favorite country song strolling through the school hallways, *"Get it up, get it on, and get on out ..."* Even his rumored behavior with high school girls were not his fault in the eyes of the local team supporters. Those girls chased him down, I suppose. But I digress.

His team ranked high in the state polls year after year. The girls' team rarely won a game. This particular year, his pretty daughter, Aurora, was a tenth grader and started on my team. Early in the season, we were competing against a much better team and remarkably, we were matching them point for point. The other team intercepted a pass and scored, then did it again. Randy yelled at Aurora to call a time-out. She did. I was livid, but set my rage aside to use the huddle productively. We lost the game by three points. In the post game talk, the girls learned not to call a time-out without my guidance.

I stewed all weekend, then first thing Monday morning, I requested a conference with Randy and the principal. I remember entering the principal's office, my heart throbbing in my temples, the cloud of Randy's cologne choking me in the tiny area. The lines I had rehearsed for two days were my only link with sanity. I delivered them, "Randy, you have a team. Don't call time-outs for mine."

Randy leaned back in the chair, crossed his ankle across his knee, picked the lint from his dress socks and chuckled. "I was afraid you'd take it like this. I was just trying to help." He chuckled again and glanced at the principal who was staring at the top of his desk.

I pointed a shaky finger at Randy and shot two word bullets between gritted teeth, "Don't help." I don't know what happened next because I left and went back to class. Randy never called another time-out from the bleachers and he gave me some space. Did I overreact to his behavior? Maybe. But I avoided a worse scenario, my players looking to the stands for advice instead of to me.

*Coaching Tip*
*Ignore most advice.*

# The Last Frontier

When Alaska is referred to as "The Last Frontier," the name could easily refer to the equity of rural Alaskan women in sports. Although Alaskan women thrive and advance in many areas of life – Alaska has a female governor, several professional female athletes and their share of female CEOs, there remains considerable room for gender equity improvement in interscholastic sports.

Federal regulations are very clear in stating that athletic programs for girls and boys must be equal. On the state level, the Alaska School Activities Association, governing body for Alaskan school sports, locks federal and state statues in place in a 221-page handbook detailing regulations for practice and play, eligibility, and tournament for all sports. Local school district contracts do not distinguish between coach's salaries depending on gender. All are very positive steps towards athletic equality, but incomplete without school level understanding and enforcement.

Usually, school changes are triggered by one person or by a small group who recognize an unfair situation and have courage enough to speak out for change. A coach plays a crucial role in leading discussions that change patterns of inequity. For instance, game times have been unfair for years. In rural areas, teams must fly to play basketball at other schools. Planning games on both Friday and Saturday nights often helps offset this expense. If there is a junior varsity team in addition to the varsity, then the game schedule begins at 4PM and lasts until 11PM. The girls' junior varsity contest commonly begins the basketball marathon, then the boys' JV game, then the varsity girls, and finally, the varsity boys. Parents and other relatives of JV girls have had to take off from work every Friday of a home game weekend to watch their girls play. Parents of boys did not. The finale game had been a boys' match for years in Barrow. It seemed to imply that the boys competed at a higher level. Not

so. The girls and their coach appealed to the principal to alternate game times each night, so they could play the "nightcap" every other game and he agreed. The coach of the boys' team reacted strongly. "Over my dead body," he yelled to that girls' coach. He sent the boys to convince the girls to withdraw their request. The use of peer pressure worked, the girls backed down. The principal stood behind his decision and starting in 2006, the girls and boys programs alternate game times on Friday and Saturday evenings. Now, it is the norm.

Likewise, athletic directors have the power to balance the treatment of boys and girls. One example is young Jason Hofacker, the athletic director for the Anchorage Christian School. Mr. Hofacker and the ACS Boosters Club put on a basketball invitational extravaganza every year during the Christmas holidays. The tournament program looks a bit different than those found in public schools. The multi-colored booklet includes advertisements for churches, Bible verses, and prayers along with team photos and rosters in addition to the three-day bracket of games. Every year, it ends with the 8:30 PM "Boys Championship" on Saturday night. My girls played in the 7:00 PM girls' championship one year and left the court as the band entered to play the national anthem for the boys. The girls were outraged, especially senior Whitney Congdon. "What the heck?" "Why didn't the band play for the girls?" "So cheap." "We are Americans, too!"

As I handed our thank you note to Mr. Hofacker the next morning, I asked, "Why wasn't the national anthem played for the girls' title game?"

The smile left his face and he answered with one word, "Tradition." I shook my head and said no more.

When Barrow's Lady Whalers returned the following year, we settled in to watch the girls' final game; we weren't participating in it this time. Wide-eyed, we watched the band set up and the spectators rise to their feet. The national anthem was played for the girls' game! My returning players chattered among themselves about how great this new process was. I was thrilled, too, but thought it was sad that we were so excited. This should have been the standard procedure all along.

I caught the ACS athletic director in the hallway later and told him how happy the playing of the song made us. Jason shrugged. "I thought a lot about what you said last year." We shook hands. I imagine he had taken some grief for changing the agenda and admired his fortitude. Another tiny step for

womankind. The argument to change to alternating championship game times will begin next year.

School funding for teams should be equal. If boys have been provided personalized shooter shirts to wear at the game, the girls should have them, too. If the boys lose half of their warm-ups outfits and have to buy new ones with school money, the girls should get new ones as well. If the girls hold fund-raisers to earn enough money for new duffle bags, the boys need to exert the same effort, not expect a handout from the school. All these scenarios have happened in recent years in Alaskan villages. Because someone spoke out, these injustices have ended.

Subtle differences occur between sports offered for males and those offered for females. In spite of more understanding and more often enforced laws, the daughters of Alaska don't always have opportunities equal to Alaska's sons.

Girls are less likely to have adult basketball role models of their own gender. Of the twenty-four girls' basketball teams throughout Alaska that advanced to the state tournament last spring, there were ten teams with female coaches and fourteen with male coaches. In those same schools, there were five female athletic directors and eighteen males. A review of the twenty-four boys' teams appearing at the state tournament reveals that there were twenty-four male head coaches. Of the forty officials at the state tournament last year, only two were women. Alaskan girls need more female role models in coaching, officiating, and athletic administration.

Gym time is limited in tiny Alaskan villages. The girls' team often practices at times that the boys don't want. Arguments are made that the boys need to practice after school to stay out of trouble or the men's coach can't leave his family before school forcing some girls to practice at 6AM or late at night. Sometimes, the boys' team is simply the favored program and gets first choice of times. Ideally, teams would rotate prime after-school or early evening practice times, but it doesn't always happen.

According to Title IX of the educational amendments of 1972, there must be equal opportunities for members of both sexes. When a sport is offered that exists primarily for boys, it must correspond financially with coaching staff, scheduling of matches, equipment and accessibility to the competitive facilities to a sport primarily for girls. Seemingly unreasonable comparisons have been accepted in Alaska. For example, football (with 30 male participants and construction of a field) has been equated to cheerleading (with six female participants who practice in the hallway). Wrestling (with 25 male participants) doesn't have to have a matching sport for girls because girls are allowed access to the team. The basketball reality in many Alaskan schools is that the boys play more games than the girls. Some schools deliberately fail to list boys' games on the official schedule so the number of games appears to be the same.

Girls that participate in sports in Alaska deserve the same opportunities as their male classmates. "The Last Frontier" should remain the romantic slogan of Alaska's true pristine wilderness and natural beauty, not gain a reputation as the catchphrase for old-fashioned biases.

*Coaching Tip*
*Speak up for the girls.*

# Coach of the Year

Soft-spoken Ryan Myers was tempered by fire and ice during his initial years of coaching in Alaska. Flames fueled by the intensity of small town basketball and the frostiness of public opinion hardened Coach Myers into a focused, successful basketball coach.

Ryan's day job is teaching math at Barrow High School. He became the girls' varsity coach the same year he began teaching here: he was a new white teacher, a double minority in Barrow, and he and his wife arrived in the village with a five-month-old baby, Felix. Life seemed full to the brim. Added to the new role as dad at home, he was a varsity coach for the first time and was in his first year of coaching girls. And he was young. So young that inspiration for his love of basketball came from his home state Oregon's Trail Blazers during his childhood, the years of Clyde "the Glide" Drexler.

I asked him what prepared him best for coaching, knowing that professional preparation and courses like Coaching Principles 101 are woefully lacking in practical application. He cited all the ways that he had worked with kids – swimming lessons, boys and girls club, YMCA, and classroom teaching. While living in London he coached young men's grade level teams, but he noted that Alaskans are much more serious about basketball than the English.

He would have noticed the intensity since he led the Barrow girls during superior seasons. The home team crowds filled every space in the gym. Ryan replaced me as varsity coach. I lost a state championship my final year. In his first season of coaching varsity, he had won a state championship and been named Alaskan "Coach of the Year." I congratulated him that year via email and his response, "It's not like I taught them everything they know," made me smile. The truth is that all coaches need to give a bit of positive credit to those they follow – generally all the former coach gets is the blame for bad habits

of players. Ryan ended his second year by advancing to the state championship, then losing the final game.

We discussed his first two years in the coach's chair. He felt he had met his expectations both years but admitted that the second year was a much better time for him; the team who finished second played more like a team, players were more sensitive to one another, and had less drama and more fun. The first year's team, the one inherited from me had good fundamental skills, but had internal strife common to teenagers plus a star trying to find her path, sometimes at the expense of others.

I wanted to know more about the moment he knew the state competition was lost. (I knew at halftime in my championship game and we were ahead, but our verve was gone; our heads were not in the game.) He shook his head slowly and looked away when I asked him when he knew the game was lost. Then, without meeting my eyes, as if he was ashamed of the memory, he quietly spoke, "There were about two minutes left and we were 20 points behind. I called a time out and told them the game was over. I told them I appreciated their efforts and that I would be subbing in for the seniors one at a time to get everyone in the game." There was a pause in our conversation, sort of a respectful moment of silence at the remembrance.

The long season matches the long Arctic winter, and one of his challenges was to endure through the thousands of miles of travel and to keep practices and time spent together interesting for the players. In contrast, his time was jam-packed with significant events. The defining moments of his coaching experience, in his mind, were when he disciplined a group of players who had broken curfew on a trip and when he told a player to quit after she refused to go into a game. He felt those two actions clearly established his expectations and identity as the team's coach. He didn't mention the abuse hurled at him from the bleachers during games or the inevitable racist conversations in which parents either want the native "daughters of Barrow" to get more playing time, or the South Pacific Islanders to get more playing time, or the solitary white kid to get in the game. I heard the under-the-breath vulgar names he was called by unsatisfied parents and was told of incidents with school administrators who supported him less than they supported his critics. He endured it all.

I had visits and phone calls from some of the players which I treasured, but their complaints were part of a pessimistic

game. I wouldn't play. My answer to every negative statement, was, "Well, he's the coach, get used to it." I refused to attend any game his first year but listened to every minute of the radio broadcast. I felt he and the players needed space from the old coach, at least that's what I would've wanted.

Ryan knew that the criticisms were all part of the job. His wife alleged that some of the fans were negative even when he won the championship and that they didn't know or appreciate how much time he'd spent at practice, researching plays, and hashing out strategies. Ryan laughed and agreed, noting that he probably made less than spare change an hour, he could never please everyone, he must truly love the game!

When asked what tip he would give new coaches, he spoke with a force that contradicted the gentle bouncing of his young son on his knee, "Ya gotta stick with what you know and not get caught up in community politics or the emotion of parents. Block out the public response and do what you know is right." His tone and strength belied the pain that information cost.

The legacy Ryan wants to leave his players? "Hopefully, they'll know I had their best interest at heart and I did my best. I want them to know I tried to be fair, and to remember that basketball is, more than anything else, fun."

It is rare that the old coach gets to listen to her replacement. I treasured the hour I spent in his living room interviewing him, realizing that even though we don't know each other, have never exchanged more than a sentence or two, our connection was a strong one, forged through the girls we coached, the game, and the unique surroundings of village life in Alaska.

*Coaching Tip*
*Coaches are all on the same team.*

# State!

In Scotland, students are released from school for "tattie days" to help harvest potatoes. Schools in the eastern United States dismiss for deer hunting season. Alaskan school districts have a different event to consider as they plan their calendars – the Alaska State Basketball Tournament held every March.

Small participating schools might as well close because most of the community travels to Anchorage for the week-long event. Empty classrooms and closed businesses state-wide in March testify to the exceptional popularity of "state."

Whispers begin among members of every basketball team early in the season, "This year, we are going to state." Coaches ask players, "Are you willing to work hard to get to state?" and they know the answer before the words leave their mouth. Everyone I've ever met that is associated with high school basketball in Alaska responds just like the players, as if they were at a pep rally, with a resounding, "YES!"

The hope of "going to state" is huge for Alaska's young athletes, especially for those in the villages. What gives the state basketball tourney the power to inspire youngsters and their communities year after year? And why, amazingly, does no one leave "state" disappointed with the quest? Only one team wins, of course, but the magic of simply being part of the event is enough. Attempting to define this magic is slippery business. Can it be analyzed by separating it into one unit of mystery with equal amounts of chance and intent, and a dollop of intense relationships and another of immense affection? I think it is as simple as the place and the sport capturing the imaginations of all the people who take part. Whatever the reason, in Alaska, going to "state" embodies an extraordinary experience for those who attend.

The Alaska State Tournament is like other states' end-of-season competition in that it focuses on the celebrated sport of basketball and carries the dreams of every kid who wants to be

the best. Basketball is big in Alaska and so is excellence. Both are motivating factors. So is excitement. Every state tournament's location tingles with anticipation as the games begin, but not quite like it feels in Alaska. Unlike the hot, crowded, standing-room-only venue of smaller states, the sprawling, colorful Sullivan Arena in Anchorage offers a circus tent atmosphere. The building is enormous enough to host two games played simultaneously on the ground floor.

Music fills the air between games. A crew of Alaska Secondary Activities Association volunteers wearing matching maroon vests scurry everywhere, competently coordinating the activities. Concessions – sellers of souvenirs, photographers, and sporting good stores – operate booths on the upper levels. An army of custodians in bright green shirts monitor the spills and litter. Meeting rooms, spacious hallways, and open spaces in the corners provide places for conversation and row after row of bright yellow and orange seats guarantee nearly eight thousand spectators a comfortable place to watch the games.

The space for fans is important because part of the magic comes from the people. Their presence cost much in effort and in dollars. Team followers can't drive to Anchorage unless they live on the relatively limited road system: the Fairbanks area, the Mat-Su valley, the Kenai Peninsula, and, of course, Anchorage. For everyone else, traveling is more difficult – they must ride the ferry or buy a plane ticket. They must stay in a hotel room and rent a car or hire a cab and buy a ticket for the games. Yet, they come. By the thousands. They bring home-made signs. They roar. Their cheering impacts the outcome of games. They support the boys and girls they have watched grow up playing in muddy streets and snowdrifts of their home town.

The emotional intensity rocks at court level while upwards in the big beehive of activity, people are visiting and eating and relaxing until their team plays. It is often a time of reunion with former village residents who have moved to more urban areas. I remember seeing many old friends who had left Barrow years before. Alaska is really a small state when it comes to tightly-knit families. Almost everyone has relatives in Anchorage or Fairbanks and they will all be there to share the excitement if a cousin or niece or nephew is playing ball. And the current village residents are there – often there are more residents of a small town in Anchorage for the tournament than there are back at home!

Boisterous crowds of out-of-towners pour into Anchorage that week and fill the hotel rooms and restaurants and shopping malls. They come from far smaller, simpler places. The novelty of the big city grabs the attention of every villager, especially kids. Differences between life in a village of 300 or even 3,000 people with Anchorage and its population of 300,000 is mind-blowing. Sometimes, participation at the state tournament is the first trip to the big city for players. For Benny, a skinny kid from Pilot Station, the trip gave him his first opportunity to ride in a car. He had driven four-wheelers and snow-machines and boats, but had never been in a car. Students regularly see their first escalator, and order fast food for the first time. For students from isolated areas, the malls are like Disneyland, the stuff of television. For some, the game of basketball is the most familiar part of the trip.

The brackets are set the week before the competition begins, eight teams for boys and eight teams for girls in four classifications, totaling sixty-four teams of twelve players each (768 teenagers!) plus coaches, plus cheerleaders and mascots, plus family members and friends. There is seldom any assurance of a win at state. Anything can happen. Sweat, tears and incredibly well played basketball are among the few sure things. It's also a good bet that upsets will happen, buzzer beaters will be shot, and Alaska's kids will play hard.

The tournament structure gives players the opportunity for basketball memories that will last a lifetime. A modified double elimination schedule is used allowing teams who lose the first game to continue playing. A losing team can't win first place, but they can keep competing for third place or beyond. Players are made to feel special – an unseen announcer with a booming voice introduces each participant by name and number as the game begins and they run onto that huge gym floor. For some of my girls, it was the scariest part of the whole experience. Professional photographers take at least one shot of each player as they are introduced and lots of action shots later. The photos are on sale upstairs for the rest of the week.

"Most Valuable Player" trophies are awarded immediately after each game from a podium at center court to a player from each team. There are free throw shooting contests and three point shooting competition for individuals complete with awards and lots of camaraderie between teams. After the championship for each classification an Olympic-like parade of all sixteen teams proceeds around the court, each school

carrying an identifying sign. Enthusiastic standing ovations greet nearly all the teams as they are announced. Trophies are presented for the highest team grade point average, sportsmanship, and the tournament runners-up and winner. The closing exercise is a compelling, emotional hour, worth the months of effort required of all participants. Those watching seem to sense the magic of the dreams of youth and applaud their potential.

There is time to debrief and reflect, the last night in the hotel and in the stores before heading home on Sunday. Classrooms the next week hum with informal discussions on fast food, the theater at the Dimond Center, descriptions of the clear elevator in the Fifth Avenue Mall, and the new friendships with girls and boys from other teams. New clothes and shoes are the norm. Playing ball, so recently the reason for living, slips a little in the priorities of youth.

Until the following fall, when practice starts and the team leader remembers and her skin begins to prickle and she whispers to her best friend, "This year, let's go to state … "

*Coaching Tip:*
*Go to state.*

# Lilly

What happens to small town Alaskan basketball stars after the end of the season? For several fevered months during their high school years, they are the focus of the hopes of a community – a high pressure role for teenagers and a challenging one to maintain to and through adulthood.

While playing, the young celebrities are the toasts of the town! Parents and family members reflect the limelight of the players. Fan clubs gather in the stands. Everyone seems concerned about their schoolwork and grades and eligibility and happiness during the season. Community members lend a hand in every way imaginable whether it is tutoring, part-time jobs, or smiling encouragement. Everyone in the village truly supports the top players.

It must be a grand feeling to be loved so much by your home town, to be the object of applause and adoration. During conversations with older athletes, I've see them smilingly drift away as they remember "back in the day." More than one high school star's life has peaked during those years, making the years after high school dark and depressing. It is hard to be a dishwasher, or a grocery bagger or unemployed with no prospects when you held the dreams of a town in your hands just the year before.

There was nothing negative or depressing in my first impression of Lilly Nungasak. When I met her, she was in her early twenties and leading the scoring on a ladies' city league team. She called for the ball often, sizzling in inevitable streaks of hot shooting in nearly every contest. In a barn-burner championship game at a tournament in Anaktuvuk Pass, I watched spellbound as she flew down the court in a bizarre surprise play to catch a full court baseball pass and score, winning the first-place trophy.

Her high school coach Martha Riley and I are friends and agreed that Lilly was one of the finest basketball players to ever

represent Barrow. With the launching of the WNBA, we speculated that she was the one woman in Barrow that could make the try-outs (if she had her head on straight).

When Lilly was in junior high, the high school boys playing pick up games in the evenings chose Lilly and treated her as an equal. Competing with older, better athletes helped hone her skills; she credits those years with teaching her the game's fine points. By the time Lilly got the high school, she could make three point shots consistently and had the crowds roaring with approval every night. Her ball-handling skills and ability to pass the ball were phenomenal. She made the All-Tourney team as a ninth grader, a rare honor and subsequently played varsity basketball successfully in Barrow for the sophomore year.

She remembers moments from her time in the public eye. One of them was in her first freshman game, firing the shot that beat Valdez by one at the buzzer. She laughed as she recalled Barrow getting thumped by them the next night. She recalled the instant the ball ripped the nets after a long three point shot to beat Monroe Catholic School in Fairbanks when she was a sophomore. After her $10^{th}$ grade season ended, her drinking became a problem that she just couldn't overcome. Lilly left Barrow as a senior for treatment at North Star Residential Treatment Center in Anchorage and graduated from East High School in 1992.

She then attended Everett College in Washington. There, Lilly held the three point scoring record and was part of a team that made their version of the play-offs for the first time in twenty years. She studied physical education and had a tough time learning from books but she was sober for five years.

Lilly reminisced about seasickness on the ferry "Olympia" in college while traveling to games. That memory caused me to marvel as I imagined all the new experiences a native girl from a little rural town would have living out of state, attending college, on her own, for the first time. She came home before she finished school.

Later, Lilly held a job with the North Slope Borough School District's alternative education program, supervising at-risk students in the workplace. She counseled. and led by example, showing students how to work hard. She volunteered as an intramural coach at the middle school level and the teams that she coached were solid in fundamental basketball skills. Then, for three years, she had the top basketball job in town, coaching the Barrow Lady Whalers. She realized that she was well known

as a basketball player and had that advantage going into the job but after the first year it became less fun. Townspeople who had been enthusiastic supporters of her as a player were critical of her as coach. Afterwards, she worked in the City of Barrow Mayor's Office. During those years, she was active as a player and team captain in the fiercely competitive Barrow City League.

After that, alcohol came back into her life hard, taking her to places she didn't want to go. She watched family members and dear friends lose their lives in alcohol-related events and her subsequent actions show that she does not want to become one of them. Lilly carefully selects her circle of friends and the places she hangs out.

I talked to her in the bleachers at a game last winter and arranged a telephone interview later to ask some questions in private. In response to "How do you want to be remembered in your hometown?" she answered, "I want people to remember that I loved basketball. I loved the challenge, the speed and the endurance it requires."

Lilly readily admits that without basketball she'd "probably be in prison for attempted murder, stealing or drug dealing" and she credits her love for both grandfathers for keeping her on the court and in the classroom. They listened to her play when games were broadcast on the radio but they never watched in person. Her elementary PE teacher also played a huge role in her love of the gym and her ambition to be a teacher.

For now, sixteen years later, Lilly is at home. She looks out for the teenagers in town that are drinking, talks to them straight from her experiences and offers her home as a safe haven whether they are drunk or sober. She means every word she says. Her warm smile and distinctive laugh underline Lilly's sincerity. I enjoy it when we can sit and visit at ball games, part of the invisible bonds of women who sit in those Whaler bleachers.

Her goals have changed over the years. Now, the most important concern for Lilly is to take care of her mother and the girls, a much younger sister and a niece, and to be there for them. Both the girls are ball players, and if you look closely, you can see Lilly's mannerisms as they shoot. They, too, will probably be leading scorers for the Whalers. Sadly, they too will probably be tempted by alcohol.

Along with the basketball education she will give them, I hope Lilly can give them more help than she got towards a smoother life, one that allows them to shine as brightly in life after the last buzzer sounds in their senior basketball season.

*Coaching Tip:*
*Consider your players' lives*
*beyond the game.*

# Little Dribblers

The Little Dribblers' basketball season began with a draft. Coaches who each had a list of second, third and fourth graders took turns picking names. I didn't know many of the children, so I chose appealing names: Bobby Pico, Jazzie, Kent, Skipper, and Hunter. These were names that fairly delighted the tongue. Perhaps not a brilliant coaching strategy, but a fun one.

A few weeks before the season, I had been hired at the local middle school as the girls' basketball coach. Even though the previous season had been near perfect in my mind, my job ended abruptly. The macho, first-year, all-knowing athletic director decided to "evaluate" coaches according to the number of wins during the season. Prior to this development, our meetings in his office consisted of me asking questions or demanding action while he rearranged piles of papers on his desk or turned his back to me and realigned books in the shelves. When I asked him when he was planning to order uniforms for the girls, he sipped his coffee and grunted, "No time soon." My lengthy speech on the problems of a troubled young female athlete was met with a muttered, "Time for her to grow up," as he examined his fingernails. My excitement in the growth that girls were making on the court and in the classroom were answered with, "Just as long as we keep winning."

I had been coaching basketball before he was born and, possibly the ultimate indignity to him, I was ten inches taller. I was also a woman. For my part, I resented the way he dismissed girls and their athletic programs as unimportant. Finally, he had a photo of his father on display in his office but not one of his mother. Both were living and devoted to him – I asked around.

I have an uncontrollable physical reaction to unfairness: my neck and face flush even before I can put my finger on exactly what is unfair. I felt the heat rising up my face whenever I even thought about this guy. His misguided attempt to equate

coaching success at a middle school level with a number of wins also made me red-faced. I figured he had given the whole process about ten seconds of thought, so I one upped him and quit the coaching job in half that time.

Due to my brilliant decision-making skills, I was without a coaching job and at loose ends for several weeks when a radio announcement caught my ear. The City of Barrow's Little Dribblers program needed coaches. I signed up, participated in the draft and found myself with a team of children each possessing a delightful name.

My team, the "Stingers," was eye-catching when they assembled for the pre-season team picture. No two players looked alike. Several players sported colorful NBA athletic gear made of expensive knit dazzle-cloth, some showed up in tattered jeans and some wore summer clothing more fitting for the beach. The variety extended to skin color, body type and personality. It seems African-Americans, Samoans, Alaskan Natives, Filipinos and white kids all have darling names. Some were extremely tall, some abnormally small and one was quite heavy. The Stingers featured exuberant, sullen, apathetic and sad children. It took considerable coaching talent to even line them up for the photographer. I blocked the mental pop-up vision of Drew smirking.

Jazzie was so shy and sad that she rarely spoke. Her parents dropped her off at the door for every practice and game but no one ever stayed to watch. She always had plenty of money to spend at the concession stand, often buying drinks and snacks for those who asked or who were standing nearby. Her innocent nature was not a good match for competitive basketball. I had watched, red-faced, the previous year as her coach directed her to a spot on the court far from the basket where she was to stand so she wouldn't get in the way of the more talented

players. Instead of slinky knit NBA short pants, her basketball shorts were made of pink cotton, with ironed creases and tiny pockets in which she kept a folded tissue and her money.

Kent made up for Jazzie's quiet. He fancied that he knew a great deal about basketball and shared his knowledge constantly. Mentally, Kent was quite a player. However, his nine-year-old arms and legs weren't working in the same direction yet. Frequently, as he learned to dribble, the ball knocked his glasses off or bloodied his nose. Both of his spectacled parents sat on the front row of the bleachers every week, taking pictures. They called out lots of advice for their son. Kent was pleasant and would push his glasses up and smile and pose for the camera during the game, even while he had the ball.

Skipper's personality was the opposite. He cried when I took him out of a game, he cried when I put him into a game. Sometimes, he just couldn't stand being on the bench and would go in to play without permission. Sometimes, he couldn't stand being on the court and left the game without permission. He was so tiny and so angry that unkind fans laughed at him. The not-so-funny part was that family members were never present to help him cope so he pressed his face against the gym wall and cried. All the misery was not internal; Skipper's face and arms were covered with oozing, itching eczema. He did have natural athleticism and incredible energy. When he worked past the tears and got in the mood to play, he was a scrapper. No rebound escaped him, and he could sense weakness in his opponents and swoop in and steal the ball at will.

Unlike Skipper, Hunter was calm and motionless and large. For much of his childhood, Hunter had been in a lower body cast. He had fallen out of an upstairs window as a kindergartener and dislocated both hips. The doctor had recommended sports to help rehabilitate his leg muscles. Hunter was good-natured but never in a hurry. It was almost as if he had forgotten he could move. He was the youngest child of a marriage that spanned two decades and six big brothers and sisters. His mom and dad were comfortable spectators. They came early armed with healthy snacks and sat one behind the other in the stands so the lower person could recline back on the knees of the partner above. They quit laughing and chatting with other parents to jump up and cheer for Hunter every time he was in the game. They even bought matching t-shirts for the team so we could have a uniform.

Bobby Pico was the source of talent for our team. He was still deciding if he was right-handed or left-handed and practiced shooting with both. He could dribble, had perfect shooting form and worked hard to improve. I suspected that Bobby got his skills and work ethic from his dad who sat on the back row keeping score in a tiny spiral bound notepad. Mr. Pico usually wore his work coveralls to the weekday practices making him seem even larger than he was. His size was tempered by the gentle way he helped Bobby take off and fold his thick winter parka before every practice and game. He didn't have much writing to do at the games; the team was not a scoring powerhouse in the Little Dribbler league.

It was a long four months. The echoes of basketballs bouncing and children shrieking in the large city gym, so exciting at the beginning of the season, were nerve wracking during the final weeks. Adults hurried past the concession stand; the sweet smells of bubblegum and soda syrup that once beckoned had become unappetizing. Even the fans had lost enthusiasm. Of course there was wild cheering whenever we scored since that was still pretty rare. Mostly people were just waiting for games to be over to take their kids or little brothers and sisters home.

Although the score wasn't officially displayed, we knew who was winning each game. Not us. Not until the last game. During that game, we completed several passes. Bobby Pico's talent for scoring began to show. Kent learned how to dribble. Skipper entered and exited the game legally. Hunter ran. We had jelled as a team and the momentum was ours! But, there was a casualty as our competitive dynamics improved. Meek Jazzie wasn't getting to touch the ball and she was sadder than usual.

The game was nearly over and we were ahead. The scoreboard was not on, but we knew. If we could only hold on for a few more seconds ... then, shockingly, Jazzie called a time-out. Everyone ran to the bench (not to the concession stand or to mom; more notable progress). We huddled and high-fived and I turned to Jazzie for the time-out rationale. She dug in her shorts pocket, brought out a tiny chain with a charm attached, held it up and asked, "Do you like my bracelet?" The team, to a player, stared at her incredulously, every mouth open. I fought my own mental eye roll and was able to nod, "The loveliest I have ever seen." She glowed and returned it to her pocket for once in good spirits.

I guess the game continued. I'm certain poor Drew would have noted the final score but I did not. We finished the last few seconds of the game but memories of who did what with the basketball vanished forever, totally erased by a little girl's smile and the gem of the day, that children need to be valued and not just for their skills with a basketball.

Slam-dunk for Jazzie.

*Coaching Tip:*
*The world is bigger than the current game.*

# Letter to Mom

March 25, 2006

Dear Mom,

My girls' basketball team lost the Alaska state championship this afternoon. It was a long game and my coaching role didn't end on the court. I hugged all the crying players afterwards, whispered comforting words to each girl and wiped their tears. We went out to dinner tonight and visited with parents who thought this or that about the game. The noise and foolishness at the restaurant was borderline inappropriate but a good emotional release for them all. The waitresses couldn't believe that we kept eating and ordering more food. We didn't want to leave. I think we all wanted to delay bedtime and the inevitable reflection on the game.

Ahhh, when I close my eyes, I can still hear that gym. The crowd roared for us. The fans from our little village are the loudest in the state and everyone from tiny Barrow who had ever moved to the big city of Anchorage was there to support their home team. You could feel the nervous energy in the cheers. Parents were nervous for their daughters. Fans wanted us to bring back the first ever Barrow state basketball championship trophy. I thought the noise in that big arena would bother the girls and me, but for me, it was like turning the radio dial, I could tune in to whatever sounds I desired. I chose the sounds on that huge court, the squeak of sneakers, the ball bouncing on a wooden floor, the buzzers, the refs' whistles, and the banter of young women.

My girls played well the first quarter, but after that we became a team of Cinderellas, running from the ball (as sad as I am, that joke still slays me). I pretty much knew it was coming at halftime, even though we were ahead by six points. The girls were silent, so tense that they couldn't tease or talk or even smile. Sure enough, we came out in the second half shooting

poorly, passing horribly, looking to get rid of the ball instead of being productive with it.

We didn't get beat, Mom, we LOST. I called time-out after time-out to try to come up with the magic words. The ones I used, "Calm down." "Play your game," "Be yourselves," did not work. Another first for me, I ran out of time-outs. Was it some weakness in me that I couldn't get the girls to relax? I still don't know what I should have done.

Besides losing, the very worst part is that I didn't get all the players in the game. Four substitutes did not play. The range of talent is considerable on the team. While there was hope, I just couldn't take a chance. With less than a minute left, the assistant coach said I would be insulting the scrubs by putting them in. I wish I hadn't listened to her and had played them all. Even angry parents complaining will be far less painful than my own conscience.

Our senior center fouled out with three minutes left. She was bawling and I was, too. We just held hands on the court until the minute allowed for substitution was over. The team captain, and the best basketball player I have ever coached, was dreadful. As it became more apparent that we were heading to a loss, she fell apart more and more, yelling at her teammates and scowling at me in frustration. The other players expected her to take over and change the momentum and her usual magic was just not there. I've coached her since 6$^{th}$ grade but she'd never been in a situation of such intense pressure so I didn't know how she would react. Hours later, she was smiling and joking, seemingly relieved. She will have another chance at a championship. Seniors Sarah and Bekah and Vanessa will not. Their quest for an Alaska basketball championship ended today. Young players Julieanna and Jen and Ashley played hard until the buzzer, no excuses, and no complaints. The team's future is in their hands.

I remember your stories of playing basketball in the 1930s in a country school back east. My favorite story is the first game in which the uniforms changed to knee length from mid-calf length. We laughed at the images of all the farmers packed in a hot, dusty gym, standing room only, in hopes of seeing a flash of flesh between knee socks and pants. Some things have changed! I require shirts over sports bras for practice but, honestly, the boys wouldn't look twice if we practiced in bras. My players show more skin in their school clothes than in a basketball uniform.

Have young women changed, too? Are our girls so pampered that when things don't go their way, they quit? Have we treated our athletes differently and created spoiled children who can't cope when they don't get their way, even with something as small as the outcome of a game? I'm pretty sure sports are overrated. I know in the grand scheme of things, state basketball championships are not the most important life event but I have to believe that the way we handle competition is significant.

I hope you would have been proud of my efforts. The team had a great season, twenty-four wins and two losses. I never lost my temper, even when frustrated. I looked everyone in the eye, win or lose, and I choked back some angry words. The "good judgment" that you often emphasized and that I lacked for many years did surface from time to time. Instead of shaking hands with the winning coach of that last game, I pulled my hand back and hugged him. It was a sweaty hug, suit jackets forced back from the intense contact but it felt right. My principal shook my hand afterwards. I considered it a great compliment, the ex-Marine shaking hands with the ex-hippie. He had been guarding the bag of state championship tee shirts stashed behind the bench for the girls. I bought them before the season with hope and laughter, knowing we had a chance, but taking nothing for granted.

Before the game, we placed three long-stemmed roses on three empty spaces on our bench. Two were for Barrow graduates, Lauren and Jodie, both ballplayers who had passed away tragically in the past two years. The girls and I knew them both and we needed to honor and remember them.

One rose was for you. I told them how grateful I was that you had allowed me to be a little different and had guided me to become the person I am.

Thanks, again. Love,

Becky

*Coaching Tip*
*Stay grounded – talk to your mom.*

# Compassion

Participation in basketball provides many opportunities to acquire positive qualities such as cooperation, confidence, and compassion. All competitive sports demand cooperation and confidence of its champions, but compassion transcends the win-or-lose world and hovers in a realm above.

Displays of compassion set a coach, a player, or a team apart from the ordinary. These events are often remembered longer than the headlines. Likewise, the absence of compassion on the court remains in the memory of those who watch.

I have been haunted for many years by one team who displayed a heinous lack of mercy. Their cruelty resulted in one non-negotiable rule I set for my teams. My team could not beat a team by more than 20 points plus we wouldn't ever let the opponent know that was our rule. In good years, we sometimes had to shoot only left-handed or shoot only three pointers or take only one dribble. It is no fun to get beaten badly. It takes the joy out of sports. I know this from a memorable first hand experience.

We had traveled about a thousand miles to play against an unnamed school in their loud gym. The lines on the court were red; the mats on the end wall were red, as were the bleachers, and even the railings in the balcony. The noise of screaming voices, horns, and the pep band quite deafened us. The gym was intimidating, but not as overwhelming as the team we were facing. The Barrow team members possessed many talents, but basketball wasn't one of them. Conversely, the opposition included two all-state players returning from the previous year. We had one starter returning. They were undefeated. We had five wins and ten defeats. Oh, and it was homecoming at their school. The bright red gym had every bleacher filled with a hometown supporter except ten seats on the bench behind us where our small entourage of parents and friends sat.

Details from the first three quarters have mercifully escaped my memory, but the last quarter remains vivid. We were behind 90-33. All but three of our players had fouled out. The two all-staters remained in the opponent's line-up along with three other starters.

Between third and fourth quarters, I gave up my time with the team to go ask the other coach if he would play only three players, to make it a bit more interesting, at least. He laughingly refused and I walked back to our bench, dejected. I sent in the three remaining eligible players and sat down to watch. My girls failed to be fast enough to even catch up with the other team's players to foul them. The red-clad athletes just passed the ball and continued to score. We'd inbound the ball, they'd double team our players and steal the ball back and score again. They ran a hundred on us without breaking a sweat. The opposing fans were sympathetic and began to leave. They seemed to have had enough of the inhumanity, too.

I refused to pull the team off the court or have girls feign injury to end the humiliation, but both thoughts crossed my mind. My three girls finished the game, a testament to their dedication. The final score was 140-33. Players and coaches shook hands afterwards but the traditional muttered "Good game" sounded empty.

We trudged to the locker room, absolutely devastated. The girls changed clothes without horseplay. The uniforms smelled bad, partly from perspiration and deodorant, but the rancid pile of damp jerseys and shorts had a stronger scent than that of body odor. If I hadn't loaded them in a duffle bag, I think the girls would have been content to leave them there. The van ride

back to Anchorage and the hotel took an hour, one of the darkest and loneliest of my life. That memory will never fade.

Neither will the equally powerful demonstration during another game years later. Victoria, an end-of-the-bench substitute, made the crowd gasp with her selflessness. She hadn't played much during this, her sixth grade season with the Hopson Middle School Wolves. Her coordination had not quite caught up with her large frame but her spirit was as big as the gym. She was new to competitive sports and didn't possess an ounce of malice. HMS led by two points late in the game and Victoria was dribbling the ball. Poorly. The opposing guard attacked again and again with near successes. Victoria seemed unaware, possibly because she watched the ball with every time she touched it.

Finally, the guard dove for the ball, missed and lost her balance and fell, skidding hard across the slick, dusty, wooden floor. The loud crash got Victoria's attention. Her face fell, instantly distressed. She tucked the ball under her arm and walked several yards over to the downed comrade. Not dribbling. Victoria offered the other girl her free hand to help her up. The crowd was incredulous. Her action ended cheers mid-syllable, leaving mouths open and an audible intake of air by the spectators. Then the air seemed to glow from the warmth radiating around the two smiling girls on the court. It spread to every person watching.

I was keeping score for this game and the referees looked at me as if to say "Whatta we do?" They gave the signal for an official timeout and approached the table.

Legally, the call should have been to take the ball from Victoria's team and let the other team inbound it. It was an important decision because it impacted the outcome of the game. The team that was behind could tie the game if they scored. Possession of the ball would surely help. The referees whispered and chuckled and agreed that they just couldn't take it away based on such an innocent selfless act. They blew the whistles and brought us back to the dusty reality of the game, pointed to the sideline and gave Victoria the ball for the throw in. The opposing coach didn't complain. No one did. Victoria broke the rules and a few cutthroat philosophies of basketball to take care of a fallen competitor. Everyone approved.

Both these are extreme examples. Compassion manifests itself in little ways, too. When a player tearfully fouls out, the effort exerted needs to be applauded, not the exit. Cheering at the mistakes of opposing players exhibits selfishness. As a young player shoots a free throw, it is insensitive to boo and kick the bleachers to make the most noise possible.

The official word is sportsmanship, but it is based on compassion. It promotes a good feeling that is contagious. I think it is the most important quality for coaches to model and to teach to children.

*Coaching Tip:*
*Nice matters.*

# Epiphany

Success in basketball requires confidence and confidence is not based on any rational thought or scientific knowledge. As a coach, I have preached that sermon a thousand times in hundreds of huddles and locker rooms. My words are inspired by a village coaching experience I remember, the hour I first believed.

This epiphany occurred during a Hopson Middle School intramural basketball game. I was coaching the Rug Rats. I know, a silly name, but the girls voted and Rug Rats got the most votes. The team was not exceptional except perhaps in regards to coachability. All of the girls attended practices regularly and worked hard trying to improve. They seemed to like me but I wasn't sure why. We had so much to do at practice we rarely had time to chat except about basketball skills. My theory was that although middle school students probably don't realize it, they crave structure and discipline; they want a reliable system in which to function. There was predictability at basketball practice, as in my language arts classroom, almost a minute-by-minute agenda.

Heather Dingman was one of the players. This skinny sixth grader was also in my class. She expressed her ideas well in an assigned journal and surprised me by sharing very private thoughts. She was soft spoken but smiled frequently. In the sixth grade hallway, boys and girls flocked to her side as friends, but none of those friends were on the team. She kept a bit apart from the older girls.

The Rug Rats were playing in the school championship game. This was not important in the national sports magazines, but it was in our little village, Barrow. Almost every family member of every Hopson Middle School intramural player was in the school gym that bitter cold Saturday afternoon. One of the reasons was that there were few other choices for entertainment. Another was that, traditionally, season ending

games were close. In our village, a "good" game wasn't necessarily a game we won. Our fans defined a "good" basketball game as hard-played and evenly matched.

The temperature outside was well below zero, but no spectator could bear to wear a coat in the overheated, noisy gym. It was a loud contest, the culmination of months of practice and games. The score had been close for the entire game. On the court, players dripped sweat. Those sitting high in the bleachers were drinking a lot of cold drinks. On the floor, we could hear the empty cans being tossed at the trashcan behind our bench. Overdressed babies cried continuously. There was the faint locker room aroma of stale sweat wafting back and forth from court to bleachers.

The other team, the Head Bangers, was one point ahead and the clock showed one second left in the fourth quarter. Heather had been fouled in the act of shooting and had two free throws. The first shot hit the top right corner of the backboard and bounced ten feet back. She was worried about not getting the ball up to the goal and put too much muscle behind it. The crowd stood, screaming at a decibel level far too high for me to talk with Heather. I called a timeout. Usually, timeouts are called between free throws when the other team is shooting. The mind of the shooter often starts wandering when there is extra time to think. In Heather's case, she needed some thinking time.

She trembled in the huddle. Another quiet girl on the team, Adrienne, wordlessly massaged her back. Katie and Cynthia hugged her. Young Miss Dingman had never made a free throw in a game. Maybe she had hit some in practice when she shot granny-style (underhanded), but I had never been a witness. In fact, hitting the backboard clearly showed progress to me. Our players were not likely to get a rebound and score with one second left. Heather must hit the shot to tie the game so we could continue in overtime. What to do? What words? What strategy?

I had no logical plan of action. I couldn't think of any success Heather had ever had in this situation, any hopeful reflection. There was no logic to apply here. I gave her no analysis of the physics of shooting, not the ideal trajectory of the ball's path or the amount of force necessary. Instead, I held her frail shoulders with both hands, looked her in the eyes and spoke from my heart, "In your mind, picture the ball going in the basket ... then shoot it." She relaxed and nodded her head,

ponytail bobbing. I shrugged, "Nothing to it." Our eyes stayed locked a little longer than a normal conversation required. I was filled with a feeling of peace that was not unlike a religious experience. I truly believed she could do it. Kinda like I had swallowed my own hook, line, and sinker. Bought my own bill of goods.

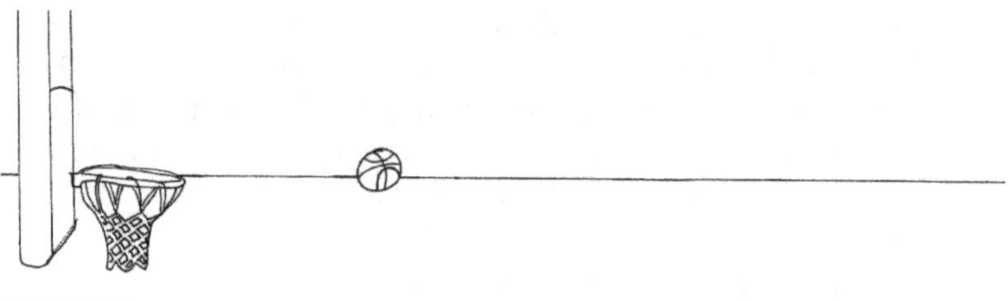

I believed. Heather believed. The girls in the huddle whooped. Gaby did a little dance. We stacked up our hands and shouted "Girl Power!" which started the crowd cheering again. My girls swaggered onto the court. With the superior wisdom of an eighth grader, Nora nodded to the fans, smiling. Katie was laughing and motioned to the crowd to raise the roof. I should have been concerned that they were too cocky. An unbiased observer would have realized that humble pie was likely to be served in approximately one second. Never occurred to me. I believed she would make the shot. No sweat beads on my brow. I can't explain why.

The girls lined up on either side of the free throw lane. One of our opponents nervously tried to retie her loose shoelace. Why was she nervous? Her team was ahead with one second left. I remained seated on the bench and motioned for the subs to sit down. We may have been the only ones in the gym not standing. Heather wiped her palms on the seat of her shorts and

reached for the ball from the referee. Then she smiled sweetly at the man. My eyes widened a bit – did she not remember to stay focused? We had spent time on the underlying theory of having a "game face."

She took a deep breath and launched the ball. The ball seemed to slow down as I watched. It was fired with way too much force, hit high on the backboard and dropped straight down where it hit the front of the rim and bounced upward. Moans began on our side of the gym. But gravity still had a say, and the ball began falling. It drifted downward where it caught the back of the rim, banged hard and .. fell ... in the hoop. The ugliest shot I have ever seen. But it counted. An explosion of screams and laughter rocked the gym. The game was tied.

We couldn't be stopped in the overtime period. The Rug Rats won the game, the championship, and all the hardware. The other teams may have been better basketball players. We simply believed.

Heather and I never spoke about that shot. She has since graduated from college and spent some time in Anchorage. Now she is back working in Barrow and we see each other by chance every few weeks. When we meet, there are always smiles and hugs. There's also a feeling of sweet connection. Ah, the power of believing in the same thing at the same moment ... the stuff of miracles ...

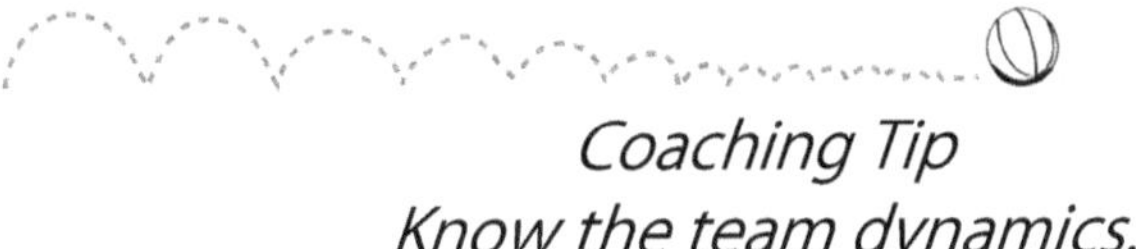

*Coaching Tip*
*Know the team dynamics.*